Body, Brain, Love

A Therapist's Workbook
for Affect Regulation and Somatic Attachment

By Karen Rachels, MFT

Graphic layout by Brad Reynolds, **www.integralartandstudies.com**

Printed in the United States of America

Dedicated to my mother, Adele Krivit Feldman,
and my aunt, Shyama Beth Friedberg

Contents

PART I – Nervous System Regulation and Dysregulation

PART II – Attachment through a Somatic Lens

PART III – An Introduction to Somatic Attachment Therapy

PART IV – Annotated Transcript and Vignettes

PART V – Tying It All Together: Body, Brain, Love

Appendices

Introduction

Welcome to the world of body-brain integration. Many of you have already been exposed to various aspects such as mindfulness and the use of the body to help contain anxiety through breathing or depression through sunlight and exercise. Common sense and well-researched medical advice all point in the direction of mental health being inseparable from physical health.

This workbook intends to take that concept and extend it into the language and practice of psychotherapy. What we understand about the brain and our ability to translate that into psychoeducation and active therapeutic interventions will make a world of difference in our clients' ability to heal from seemingly intractable wounds and behavior patterns.

I have come to believe that not knowing certain basic neuroscience can, at times, lead to an unethical practice. If a therapist cannot recognize nervous system dysregulation, clients may be re-traumatized or be left feeling or being unsafe. **Part I** provides the initial focus of this book. It specifically teaches the basic neuroscience referred to above in simple, accessible terms for direct application in the therapy room. Affect regulation through mindfulness and resourcing are essential tools in any therapist's toolbox. This part of the workbook will give you enough information to help regulate your clients. Any regulating interventions will be greatly enhanced by using the basic somatic skills of tracking, contacting, and deepening. These skills are taught in Part III.

Part II teaches attachment theory through the lens of neuroscience and nervous system regulation. Intrapersonal affect regulation often has its roots in the interpersonal regulation that did, or did not, take place in early attachment relationships. This part of the book seeks to help you apply body-brain understanding of your own and your clients' attachment dynamics. When put together, affect regulation, somatic skills, and attachment theory can influence and deepen your work in unexpected, moving ways. Ultimately, this work will help grow your clients' brains by facilitating neural connections and integrating critical brain structures.

Part III is optional and I do hope you will read it. It reflects my special invitation to you to try out the world of Somatic Attachment Therapy. Please also read the next chapter, "Invitation," if you are curious about this specific therapy approach. By reading Part III, you will gain some tools to provide a powerful, deep and transformative therapeutic experience. Having a sense of what a somatic attachment approach can look like, I hope, will answer that nagging thought you may have had, "I know there is something else there I could get to if I had the right tool." Working directly and frequently with the body can begin to answer that question.

Part IV offers substantive real-life examples of what this approach looks like in actual practice. An annotated and analyzed transcript of a Somatic Attachment Therapy session is provided as well as two vignettes by other therapists.

Part V addresses the "love" aspect of "Body, Brain, Love." In this section, I discuss the nature of love as a physiological, regulatory entity that has a fundamental place in the therapy we practice.

Finally, the Appendix contains a glossary, bibliography, resources for continued learning, and an answer key for the exercises in the workbook. In addition, the Appendix offers a Continuing Education Opportunity for licensed LCSWs and MFTs in California. A course exam and evaluation is included. Readers may also read how to order the DVD that will accompany this workbook in April, 2015.

Invitation to Somatic Attachment Therapy

After almost ten years of working mostly psychodynamically, I found myself restless and vaguely frustrated with the work my clients and I were doing together. While I felt confident that childhood patterns and subsequent reinforcement were the basis of a person's capacity for resilience to life events, my sessions felt repetitive, not quite alive, and, worst of all, not very effective. My clients and I had good relationships and we processed what came up between us; I knew that was critical for change. But, for several years I'd been feeling there was something I needed to access with more depth and resonance and, primarily, more tangible transformative change.

I heard about somatics early on in my internships following graduate school. I thought the approach was interesting but believed it didn't fit with my psychodynamic way of thinking. At least that was what I told myself: "Therapists shouldn't use techniques, per se. We need to stay with the relationship, the transference." Some of those thoughts were true to my orientation and some were a reflection of something more about myself: I was afraid to try, afraid I couldn't do it right, afraid it would turn clients off, afraid I would be too vulnerable.

Over the years, the nagging feeling that there was more powerful and satisfying work possible led me to EMDR. EMDR seemed so very different at the time I learned it. It was definitely a technique and I felt less interpersonally engaged with clients while doing the processing. It did, however, teach me some important things: 1) The body matters; 2) The capacity to heal lives within each client's mind and body; 3) As a therapist, I need to get out of the way to let that capacity come forward; and 4) I don't have to know everything: It can unfold.

After finding value in EMDR, which I still use, I sought more direct somatics training and took the Hakomi Psychotherapy Professional Skills Training. Hakomi opened doors for me that desperately needed to be opened. These were my doors as a person, not just as a therapist. In Hakomi, I learned: 1) It is not only okay but vital that I let myself love my clients; 2) Being gentle, compassionate and loving with myself was a prerequisite for being that way with clients; 3) Focusing on positive things was a fundamental part of healing; 4) "Resistance" and "personality disorders" are ways of being and behaving which enabled someone, including myself, to psychologically survive; 5) The process of therapy is a collaborative journey where the client and the therapist are both in the unknown together.

As I worked toward Hakomi certification, the stress and pressure to know and understand everything diminished, my capacity to be more myself in session grew as did my capacity to simply "be with" my clients.

Hakomi was a route to changing my life and my practice but it couldn't stop there. A given client's intense emotional lability or another client's difficulty being emotionally connected led me to study emotional and physiological regulation, trauma treatment, and attachment through a somatic lens. I took trainings in Sensorimotor Psychotherapy, Emotionally-Focused Couples Therapy, Julie Murphy's "Attending to Attachment" course, and began to study the neuroscience of attachment.

In one of the first somatics/attachment consultation groups I facilitated, I realized some students did not know about regulation. I started teaching them about recognizing dysregulation and trauma, and how to work with it with their clients. Over time, it became clear to me that not knowing about regulation put therapists and clients at risk. Clients could be re-traumatized or not feel safe. And, the path to safety (Stephen Porges' term) through attachment was not being accessed.

Jaklyn Brookman, my collaborator, was in that first group/class. After a few weeks, she said, "You need to write a workbook." Thank you, Jackie. The curriculum I was then writing on the fly became the skeleton of this workbook. I later devised the term, Somatic Attachment Therapy, to describe the work.

This workbook and, particularly Part III, is for you as a person and you as a therapist.

I have designed it to be accessible, easy to digest, and to provide just the right amount of neuroscience therapists need. I invite you to find the parts that fit—to learn about your own regulation, how your brain and your mind come together to keep you safe, relate to important others, take risks, feel joy, and play, as well as to survive trauma, grief, and the profound difficulties of our lives in a too-often inhumane world.

This particular workbook will also enable you to step at your own pace, if you choose, into the world of somatics and invite you to look at your own regulation and attachment strategies as a fundamental aspect of your relationships with clients. Attachment refines transference and countertransference; it gives us a map for the intrapersonal and inter-subjective field that is the basis for any change. Attachment with somatics gives us an active, process-apparent way of seeing what unfolds and how to change/transform in the moment.

Welcome to the alive world of Somatic Attachment Therapy. May it help you grow in ways that nourish you and your clients.

Part I
Nervous System Regulation and Dysregulation

Chapter 1

Mindfulness

We begin our study of body-brain integration by learning about mindfulness. Observation and awareness of all facets of experience is the basis for developing the choice to change and to heal. Mindfulness is a concept and practice that comes from many traditions. It has only been in the last few decades that the psychotherapy community has seen the wisdom of its use.

In mindfulness meditation, a person notices the mind, lets go and detaches from intense emotion and unattainable desires. Mindfulness can help the person witness the emotion and the grasping that leads to suffering. In Hindu practice, this is sometimes called "witnessing consciousness." Long-term mindful meditators often have a greater internal spiritual peace and a more secure psychological attachment.*

Many psychotherapies, including Dialectical Behavioral Therapy and spirituality-informed therapies, have adapted the concept of mindfulness to help the person observe and slow down the degree of control their emotions and irrational thoughts have on their lives. Such observation can help the person experience more distance from overwhelming emotions and thoughts and gradually learn to control them, resulting in more stability in their lives.

---

* See Daniel Siegel's *The Neurobiology of We* for an in-depth discussion of the psychological and physical benefits of meditation.

The kind of mindfulness you will learn in this workbook is utilized by many body-based therapies. Mindfulness becomes a practice for a person to observe their internal world. This observation facilitates the understanding of how they have organized their experiences. When talking is minimized and attention is put to other modes of experience such as physical sensations, feelings, urges, the qualities of breath, and muscle tension, the person's more unconscious experiences can be accessed.

Mindful awareness is comprised of three elements:

1. Tuning into self.
2. Observing what is happening within you while experiencing at the same time.
3. Utilizing the following body-brain tools to become our own best friend: Curiosity, Openness, Acceptance, Love (COAL – acronym and concept by Daniel Siegel in *The Neurobiology of We* – see bibliography).

Mindfulness Induction vs. Progressive Relaxation Induction

To work with clients somatically, we need to teach them how to access a mindful, observing state. In doing so, it is important to distinguish between progressive relaxation and mindfulness.

Progressive relaxation deliberately helps the person relax through suggestion as the therapist guides the person to relax each part of the body. In contrast, mindfulness aims to encourage and maintain observation and awareness of internal experience. It promotes the observation of all internal experiences including physical sensations, emotions, muscle tension, micromovements, quality of energy, urges, and shallowness or depth of breath. The goal is observation while experiencing rather than changing the experience, although the experience will change through the observation. We are not suggesting to the client that they experience anything in particular. The only exception is when the client is dysregulated, a topic I will discuss in depth later.

Below is a step-by-step guide for inducing mindfulness in the therapy room:

1. Ask the person if they want to explore what they are talking about.

2. If the person agrees, suggest a way to go inside which can include closing the eyes, having a soft gaze, keeping the eyes open but cast down, or keeping the eyes open and just listening.

3. Begin by changing the pace and tone of your voice, making it slightly more rhythmic and even rather than inflected.

4. When you speak, it is better to use language such as "Let yourself…," "Take a moment to…," "As you get more still, notice…". Use "you" rather than "we" or "us."

5. Gently direct the person to notice the physical experience they are having such as the support of the couch, feet on the ground, or changes in the cadence of your voice. Do this in a measured, rhythmic way.

6. After several suggestions like this, and as you yourself start noticing some things you hadn't noticed, start incorporating your own observations by saying things like, "You might notice the ticking of the clock, or the passing of traffic outside. Perhaps you feel a sensation of light filtering through your eyelids…"

7. Lastly, begin to direct the person inside. "Now, begin to bring your attention to what's happening inside. Whatever you notice is completely okay. There is no right or wrong; there are only things to notice and experience. Notice if there are any feelings, physical sensations, images, thoughts, urges. Take a moment to notice whatever is there. And, when you are ready, let me know what you are noticing."

Try experimenting with doing mindfulness with friends and family to gain some mastery. You can try it with clients to see how they respond, what they notice, and then fold that back into the work you are doing. Later, with other somatic skills, what comes from mindfulness will expand and feel even more useful.

Chapter 2

We are Braingrowers, Not Shrinks!

——————

Evolution has prepared us beautifully as living beings to protect against hostile, dangerous environments. Our brains and bodies are geared to seek out and respond to danger. Reptiles and mammals, living beings before we evolved, instinctively respond to danger and return to normal as the danger resolves.

As humans, the highest and evolutionarily newest of living beings, we retain that capacity to sense and respond to danger, then return to normal. Critical brain structures (described in the next chapter, "Normal Regulation") within human brains facilitate this response-recovery cycle.

As therapists, the work we do with our clients facilitates the maturation and integration of these brain structures. As part of that process, new fibers and nerve cells grow which increase the growth of synaptic connections and the size of these vital brain structures. Essential brain development that was thwarted has a chance to unfold thanks to the ongoing neuroplasticity of our brains. If we are doing therapy with care and respect in the best interests of our clients, we have a big role in this physiological unfolding. Understanding how this works will give you an opportunity to facilitate and enhance that development.

Fear without relief or recovery shrinks the brain. Therefore, if we were shrinks, we would be creating an environment of fear. In this scenario, the critical brain structures that help us feel safe do not have an opportunity to mature or integrate with each other. Fibers, nerve cells, and synaptic connections not used are and will continue to be pruned.

By contrast, **what grows the brain is intrapersonal and interpersonal safety**, and this is what we want and need to offer our clients. People who have a sense of well-being, self-actualization, and connections to others have brains that have, through their lives, integrated the communication and energy flow among their critical brain structures. Growing up in safe environments or being in a consistent, safe, and loving therapeutic environment naturally results in integrated brain structures. When continually reinforced and internalized, secure attachment is possible.

Chapter 3

Normal Regulation

Our human brain actually contains three brain structures developed through evolution which work together to respond to danger. These structures are presented here conceptually following the "triune brain" theory of Paul MacLean, explained in depth in his 1990 book, *The Triune Brain in Evolution*. Later research indicates these brains are not as discrete as originally conceptualized. For our work as therapists, however, studying them as discrete brains facilitates an easy, translatable use with clients.

Each brain reflects a further evolutionary change necessary for survival. The brains of reptiles were sufficient for the needs of instinct-driven living being. With the development of birds and mammals, where caring for, feeding, and protecting the young from predators became paramount, an additional layer of brain functioning was needed. This enlarged brain enabled the growth of attachment, social bonding, and emotional memory to ensure community survival. Humans, the most developed mammal, required a third layer of brain structure with the advent of language, abstraction, and thought. As we will see, communication and integration amongst all three brain structures is essential for overall healthy physical and emotional functioning.

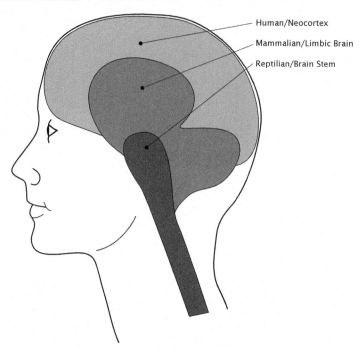

Human/Neocortex
Mammalian/Limbic Brain
Reptilian/Brain Stem

The Evolving Triune Brain

Diagram used with permission from *Buddha's Brain*, R. Hanson, New Harbinger Publications.
(Terminology modified by K. Rachels)

1. **Reptilian/brain stem** (most archaic and interior brain): senses and reacts to danger instinctually, dating back 500 million years; involved with aggression, dominance, and territoriality; basal ganglia are the most critical brain structures.

2. **Paleomammalian/limbic** (second layer of brain): emotional brain which orchestrates a nervous system and electrochemical response to danger; responsible for motivation and emotion involved with feeding, reproduction, and parental behavior.

3. **Neomammalian/neocortex** (most recent, topmost brain layer): appraising and thinking brain which facilitates a return to homeostasis; involved in language, abstract thinking, planning, and perception.

Our human brain utilizes all three sub-brains in the entire cycle of response and recovery which is called *regulation*.

Here's a fun, shorthand version of the communication between the brains during regulation:

Reptilian (to Mammalian): *Oh, something's up.*

Mammalian: *Okay, I'll send in the troops.*

Neocortex: *Wait a second, this really is okay, not a real danger, calm down.*

Mammalian: *Okay, I'll recall the troops and we can go back to normal.*

> ***Understanding regulation is the single most important concept you need to grow clients' brains.***

The healing power of therapy is amplified greatly by the therapist's capacity to help the client on a moment-to-moment basis return to regulated homeostasis.

Understanding regulation will open up many therapeutic doors for you. Take your time to understand this basic outline of regulation. It will be well worth your while.

Following understanding regulation, we will look at dysregulation and why it is the essence of what our brings clients to therapy.

Normal Regulation

Normal regulation is characterized by an electrochemical cycle of response that moves through the three brains.

We begin with homeostasis. Neurobiologically, homeostasis is the normal ***activation*** of the PARASYMPATHETIC NERVOUS SYSTEM (PNS) which functions at different points in each of the three brains. The parasympathetic nervous system, a branch of our AUTONOMIC NERVOUS SYSTEM (ANS), governs our everyday activity. This activation of the PNS is responsible for the stimulation of "rest and digest" activities, social engagement, and attachment. When everything is fine, when we are experiencing connection, relaxation, and are in the present, this part of the PNS is activated. Another important part of the PNS will be discussed later.

The PNS, as part of its job, is sensitive to threats and danger and scans the environment to make sure everything is safe. If sensory information indicating possible danger comes in from the reptilian brain (brain stem) through the THALAMUS, a brain structure that sits atop the brain stem, the SYMPATHETIC NERVOUS SYSTEM (SNS, another branch of the ANS) becomes activated.

The thalamus, beginning to activate the SNS, reads the sensory input and immediately sends a "watch out" signal to three key structures in the limbic system (mammalian brain): HYPOTHALAMUS, AMYGDALA, HIPPOCAMPUS.

The HYPOTHALAMUS starts a release of neurochemicals including epinephrine and cortisol to mobilize the body for flight or fight.

At the same time, the AMYGDALA sounds the alarm to the SYMPATHETIC NERVOUS SYSTEM, which *activates* a neuroelectrical response to mobilize the body for fight or flight.

The hypothalamus and amygdala *quickly* facilitate bodily responses to danger — sending energy to the large muscles, shutting down cognitive, digestive and immune system responses, and increasing general energy for rapid, instinctive movement. On the other hand, the hippocampus *slowly* gets the message from the thalamus and the amygdala and sends the information to the NEOCORTEX (specifically the MIDDLE PREFRONTAL CORTEX or PFC) for appraisal, discrimination and determination of the presence of real danger.

Because the hippocampus process is much slower than the hypothalamus/amygdala process, the body is already in fight or flight mode before the message gets back to the amygdala that there really isn't a danger. Once the amygdala receives this message from the hippocampus, it shuts the alarm off as it returns the body to the activated parasympathetic nervous system of "rest and digest" homeostasis and the social engagement system.

The everyday normal cycle over the course of many years leads to high-level amygdala-hippocampus connectivity such that the fight-flight and recovery process is reduced to nanoseconds.

One of our key goals as brain-growing therapists is to increase the connectivity between the amygdala and the hippocampus. Such an increase enhances the communication between the limbic system and the neocortex and facilitates rapid relief from fear.

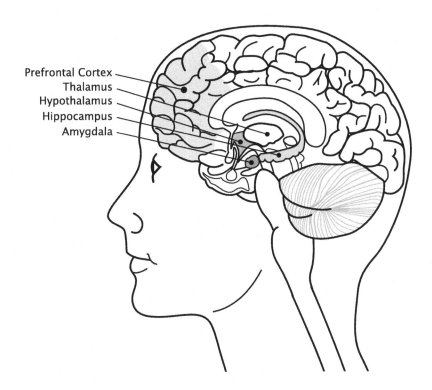

Prefrontal Cortex
Thalamus
Hypothalamus
Hippocampus
Amygdala

Limbic System — Neocortex

Diagram used with permission from *Buddha's Brain*, R. Hanson, New Harbinger Publications, p. 54.

Thalamus (to self): *I am sensing something bad that is scaring me.*

Thalamus (out loud): *Hey, Amygdala, Hypothalamus and Hippocampus: Something bad is coming down.*

Hypothalamus: *Okay, I'll send in some epinephrine and cortisol to get us ready to fight or get out of here.*

Amygdala: *Watch out! Get ready to run, nothing else matters, we're in trouble.*

Hippocampus: *Huh?*

Amygdala (panicked, fast voice): *Yeah, my legs are charged to go, I'm not hanging around and I suggest you don't either.*

Hippocampus: *What? All this stuff is happening, why?*

Hypothalamus and Amygdala: *What are you waiting for, don't you know we're in trouble? We can't wait for you.*

Hippocampus: *Trouble? What do you mean trouble?*

Hypothalamus/Amygdala (shouting): *TROUBLE!!!!!!! What's wrong with you? We can't wait for you.*

Hippocampus: *Can you calm down, please, and let me know what's going on?*

Hypothalamus/Amygdala: *NO!*

Hippocampus: *Okay, I have to send this up the chain because I'm not sure we need to do this. Hey, PFC, what do you think? Amygdala and Hippocampus are acting crazy.*

PFC: *No, I'm looking at this and I don't see it. It's just a car backfire. Tell them to calm down.*

Hippocampus: *Got it. No real danger here, right?*

PFC: *No danger.*

Hippocampus: *Amygdala and Hypothalamus, relax, there isn't anything scary happening.*

Amygdala/Hypothalamus: *Really? But I'm still scared, my body is still charged up, I can't think.*

Hippocampus: *Really. Stop the cortisol and epinephrine.*

Amygdala (beginning to breathe more slowly): *Okay, I'll turn off the alarm.*

Chapter 4

The Fear and Recovery Process of our Brains: Dysregulation

———————

Now that we have looked at the normal regulation cycle of our Autonomic Nervous System, we turn to dysregulation. Dysregulation is important to historical, evolutionary survival and continues to be important today. What's critical for us as therapists is to help clients recognize when they are dysregulated beyond what is necessary and how to return to a regulated state. This chapter will help you understand the neuroscience of dysregulation and how to work with it in therapy.

What does the Dysregulation Cycle look like?

Dysregulation results when a perceived threat or danger does not resolve. The thalamus perceives threat or danger from sensory information and begins to activate the SNS, sending the message to the hypothalamus, the amygdala and the hippocampus. The amygdala and hypothalamus mobilize the body for fight or flight by sounding the alarm bell and releasing cortisol and norepinephrine.

However, the threat is not dissipating and the amygdala/hypothalamus continue fight or flight mode. The alarm bell of the amygdala continues to ring. The hippocampus is trying to transmit the information to the PFC for appraisal but the alarm bell won't turn off, so an appraisal of safety is not possible.

Or, in extreme situations, the danger is so severe that fight or flight is not possible and the parasympathetic nervous system, through its DORSAL VAGAL NERVE, prepares the body for dissociation, freeze, or shutdown. We see this with animals when they play dead or hold their tails between their legs.

As humans, we have similar responses: Our breathing and heart rate slows, we become quiet and small, numb or frozen. The amygdala has effectively shut down the hippocampus and most bodily functions to protect us from mortal danger.

Study the graphic below to see this process in visual form.

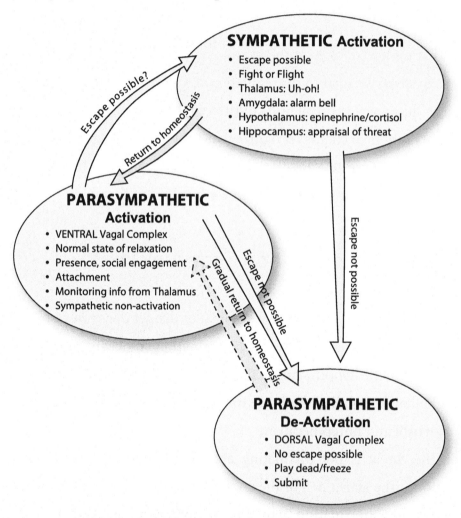

ANS Regulation and Dysregulation

Below is a graphic showing some of the bodily effects of the SNS and the PNS. Notice how the SNS facilitates fight/flight responses by dilating pupils and lungs, accelerating heartbeat, secreting adrenaline (epinephrine), and inhibiting bladder contraction and digestion. The PNS, by contrast, returns all of this to normal homeostatic functioning. The dorsal vagal branch of the PNS, however, in times of extreme life-threatening danger, distorts some of these "rest and digest" functions so that the body slows down too much and either freezes or shuts down.

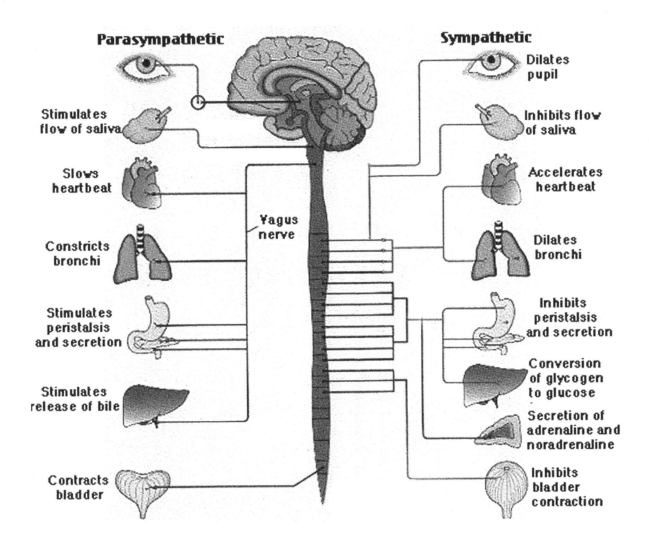

Parasympathetic and Sympathetic Physical Impacts

Finally, we go back to our major characters now starring in the play of dysregulation.

SNS Dysregulation:

Thalamus: (to self) *There it is again.*

Thalamus (outloud to amygdala, hypothalamus and hippocampus): *It's happening again.*

Hypothalamus: *Epinephrine and cortisol by the buckets.*

Amygdala: *Watch out, trouble happening again, stop thinking, start running. OMG, this is too much, can't handle this, stop it!*

Hippocampus: *You are screaming so much, you are overwhelming me. I can't understand what's happening.*

Amygdala: *Run, hit, whatever, whatever.*

Hippocampus: *I know there's a problem and I've trying to send it up the chain over and over but you keep screaming. It's making me weak and tired. I can't keep doing this.*

Amygdala (screaming): *I got this, don't need you, you're too weak and tired anyway, don't have time to think, explain to you.*

Hypothalamus: *Amygdala, here's some more epinephrine and cortisol.*

Amygala: *Oh, no, need more help, keep running, fighting, this is too much!!!!*

OR

PNS Dysregulation:

Thalamus(to self): *There it is again.*

Thalamus (outloud to Amygdala, Hypothamus and Hippocampus): *It's happening again.*

Hypothalamus: *Can't get away, can't fight. I'm shutting down, no more epinephrine or cortisol from me.*

Amygdala: *Can't get away, shhhhhh, be quiet!*

Hippocampus: *I can't hear you.*

Amygdala (quietly to Dorsal Vagal): *Can you help, please?*

Dorsal Vagal (soft, dull, fading voice): *Get small, shhhhh, very quiet, don't move an inch, hold breath, forget, forget, don't see, don't feel.*

What causes Dysregulation:
The accurate or inaccurate perception of threat

1. **Environment**

    a. Environmental sounds or visual experiences without immediate explanation: backfires; someone coming up from behind suddenly; sudden firecracker.

        Is the threat real? NO

    b. Real, discrete incidences of threat or danger to the body or the psyche: someone holding a gun to your face; a car careening front-on into your car; torture; rape; sexual or physical abuse; domestic violence.

        Is the threat real? YES

2. **Stress, acute and chronic**

    a. Acute: overwork; interpersonal difficulties; financial distress; grief; loss of job or relationship.

        Is the threat real? Not in terms of physical survival, usually.

    b. Chronic: Presence of the above stresses over prolonged period of time, unresolved, or having developed into patterns of life.

        Is the threat real? Not in terms of physical survival, usually.

3. **Life-threatening illness:**

    Is the threat real? YES

4. ***Complex or Developmental Trauma:***
    Current childhood experiences of repeated patterns of sexual or physical abuse or extreme neglect by a caregiver such that the child's psychological and physical development is directly impacted.

    Is the threat real? YES

5. ***Prolonged exposure to extraordinary threat:***
    Captivity; active combat; ritual abuse; urban settings where there is daily exposure to violence.

    Is the threat real? YES

6. ***Attachment Injury or Trauma***
    a. Attachment injury: Discrete situation whereby a caregiver's ability to be present to provide safety, comfort, play, and socialization to a child through the first 4 years is compromised, e.g., death of caregiver; hospitalization of caregiver or child; prolonged separation.

        Is the threat real? YES, from psychological standpoint.

    b. Attachment trauma: Enduring daily patterning of responses from caregiver to infants and young children that inadequately provides for comfort, safety and play during the critical, vulnerable limbic-dominant years – leads to attachment insecurity.

        Is the threat real? YES, from psychological standpoint.

7. *Implicit memory of all of the above*

Any of the above experiences that are not resolved or cannot be resolved lead to unconscious somatic memory in the limbic system of the brain.

Is the threat real? NO

8. *Dysregulation during therapy*

What happens during therapy sessions frequently activates the nervous system, trauma responses or insecure attachment responses.

Is the threat real? Hopefully, no, unless there is severe lack of attunement and/or no repair.

EXAMPLES OF DYSREGULATION IN THERAPY

◊   When a client is "triggered", their nervous system is dysregulated.

◊   When a client is uncomfortable with their own needs, they are dysregulated in terms of attachment

◊   When a client is chronically depressed or anxious, they are chronically dysregulated.

◊   When a client has symptoms of PTSD, they are acutely or chronically dysregulated.

◊   When a client cuts, they are dysregulated and trying to self-regulate themselves.

◊   When you are flustered, spaced out, or anxious with a client, you are dysregulated, possibly in terms of attachment.

MATCHING GAME

Place the number of the word next to its correct definition.

1. Amygdala

_____Brain system within the mammalian brain responsible for emotional/somatic memory

2. Hippocampus

_____"Rest and Digest" part of Autonomic Nervous System

3. Thalamus

_____Specific part of neocortex engaged with appraising danger/threat

4. Brain Stem/ Reptilian Brain

_____"Fight or Flight" part of Autonomic Nervous System

5. Mammalian Brain

_____Brain that houses the limbic system

6. Neocortex/ Neomammalian

_____Instinctive, unconscious neurobiological process of sensing threat, responding and returning to homeostasis

7. Limbic System

_____Brain structure that releases "flight or fight" neurochemicals

8. Middle Prefrontal Cortex (PFC)

_____Limbic brain structure that activates the alarm system

9. Hypothalamus

_____Limbic brain structure that communicates with amygdala and neocortex

10. Regulation

_____Oldest brain structure that instinctively responds to danger/threat

11. Parasympathetic Nervous System

_____Evolutionarily newest brain unique to humans involved in thinking, appraisal and language

12. Sympathetic Nervous System

_____Structure in brainstem that senses threat/danger and sends signals to limbic system structures.

POST-TEST: Regulation and Dysregulation

1. Human brains have three overarching brain systems that have evolved over millions of years. They are:

   a. _____

   b. _____

   c. _____

2. Name the main responsibilities of each brain system above.

   a. _____

   b. _____

   c. _____

3. The Autonomic Nervous System has two primary branches. Name each and briefly describe its function.

   a. _____

   _____

   b. _____

   _____

4. Between the limbic system and the neocortex, which one responds more quickly and more unconsciously?

5. Where is the amygdala located and what is its job?

6. When the amygdala and the hypothalamus receive the signal from the thalamus, what are some of the changes that happen in the body?

7. What is the hippocampus and how does it interact with the amygdala in a person with a normally-regulated nervous system?

    _____

    _____

8. Describe what happens in the parasympathetic nervous system in a normally-regulated person recovering from an acute stressor?

    _____

    _____

    _____

    _____

9. In your own words, describe how trauma of any kind affects the functioning of the two branches of the autonomic nervous system.

    _____

    _____

    _____

    _____

10. Two important goals for any clinician working with any client are:
    a. Help clients learn to _____ their emotional and physical states.
    b. Help clients _____ the unconscious and conscious activities of their minds.

Chapter 5

Working with Dysregulation: Window of Tolerance, Mindfulness, and Resourcing

---

How do we work with Dysregulation?

To be effective therapists, regardless of orientation or approach, we need to understand and work with our clients' dysregulation. As somatic therapists, we have several key tools at our disposal.

1. Window of Tolerance

2. Mindfulness of Somatic Experience

3. Resourcing

1. Window of Tolerance

The Window of Tolerance is a concept developed by Dr. Daniel Siegel (*www.drdaniel siegel.com*). It provides a simple way to visualize regulation and dysregulation and is easy for therapists and clients to use together. The teaching of the Window of Tolerance as a tool for dysregulation and trauma treatment was initiated by the Sensorimotor Psychotherapy Institute (*www.sensorimotorpsychotherapy.org*). "The Autonomic Arousal Model" diagram in these materials is also from the Sensorimotor Psychotherapy Institute.

Basic Window of Tolerance Model

HYPERAROUSAL (SNS)

- "Triggered"; overwhelmed
- Strong, visible stress response
- Confused thinking
- High level of emotions; rage

Window of Tolerance (PNS/SNS)

- Tolerable responses to stress
- Rest and Digest
- Being Present
- Play and Joy
- Connection/Attachment
- Homeostasis

HYPOAROUSAL (PNS)

- "Shut down"
- Strong, invisible stress response
- Thinking minimized
- Constrained emotions

In this diagram, we see three bands of nervous system activity:

a. SNS <u>activation</u> called HYPERAROUSAL
b. PNS <u>activation</u> and SNS <u>nonactivation or mild activation</u> representing the regulated, homeostatic balance we call the WINDOW OF TOLERANCE.
c. PNS <u>deactivation</u> called HYPOAROUSAL

The middle portion of this diagram shows the nervous system status accompanying normal human day-to-day experiences. We walk through life with a range of tolerance for everyday minor stresses and minor joys/excitements our nervous systems can manage. These experiences live in the middle band, the WINDOW OF TOLERANCE (WOT). In this band, the sympathetic and parasympathetic branches are working together. As noted before, this is the where the crucial social engagement system operates, mediated by the Ventral Vagal Complex of the PNS. Here there is a general feeling of safety, connection, attachment, and the ability to take risks.

When we are in the Window of Tolerance, we can think and feel at the same time. We are calm and are available for whatever we are experiencing in the present. In this state, there is appropriate SNS activity (no or minimal activation) that allows for social engagement and PNS activation that allows for rest, digestion, communication, attachment, and processing of information fully and accurately.

When we are in the WOT, our parasympathetic nervous system is activated, working properly and taking good care of us. Our social engagement system is available to us. We can play and we can take it easy. We can have intense, engaged conversations and we can be together in silence. We can face a conflict with both our feelings and our rational thoughts as sources of information.

Some minor stresses/excitements will trend to the top of the WOT band yet do not cause nervous system dysregulation.

Examples: traffic; late to work; see a person you have crush on.

Some minor stresses or situations will trend toward the bottom of the WOT band yet do not cause nervous system dysregulation.

Examples: spaced out during boring lecture; moment of grief/depression remembering a loved one who died a while ago; moderately-deep meditative state.

The diagram below shows somatic signs of regulation and dysregulation. The following page offers more information about dysregulation.

Bodily Signs of Dysregulation: Small WOT

HYPERAROUSAL (Activation)

- Shallow breathing
- Flushed face; muscle tension
- Flitting eyes; fast speech/movement
- Heart beating fast; fast speech

Window of Tolerance (PNS Activation/SNS Deactivation)

- Normal breathing
- Appears calm and present
- Easy eye contact
- Emotions available and manageable
- Engaged in relationship
- Laughter, sense of humor available

Therapist Goal:
Enlarge Window
of Tolerance

HYPOAROUSAL (PNS Deactivation)

- Very slow breathing/heart rate
- Glassy eyes, pale skin color
- Staccato, slow speech
- Little emotion

Autonomic Arousal Model
(Ogden, Minton & Pain, 2006)

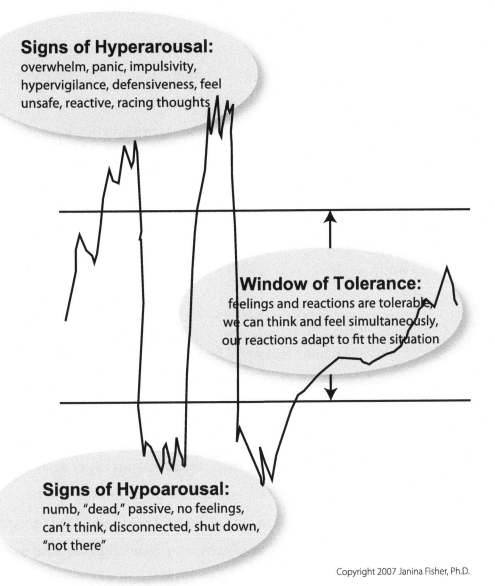

Signs of Hyperarousal:
overwhelm, panic, impulsivity, hypervigilance, defensiveness, feel unsafe, reactive, racing thoughts

Window of Tolerance:
feelings and reactions are tolerable, we can think and feel simultaneously, our reactions adapt to fit the situation

Signs of Hypoarousal:
numb, "dead," passive, no feelings, can't think, disconnected, shut down, "not there"

Copyright 2007 Janina Fisher, Ph.D.

Let's look at the top band in the diagram above. It shows sympathetic nervous system activation, HYPERAROUSAL. Pay attention to the somatic signs of SNS activation:

Panic

Racing thoughts

Fast heart rate

Quick or shallow breathing

Agitated body movements

Hypervigilance

Rage

These are the physical manifestations of fight or flight—the body trying to fight against or get away from something it perceives as threatening.

Now, let's look at the bottom band. It shows parasympathetic nervous system deactivation, HYPOAROUSAL. Pay attention to the somatic signs of PNS deactivation:

Low heart rate

Long, slow breathing

Feeling spaced out or numb

Slumped body

Dissociation

Feeling out of your body

These are the physical manifestations of freeze or submit: The body senses a threat as inescapable danger and becomes small and dead-like for maximum protection. When we are in the WOT, our bodies are attuned to actual danger. From that space, they can detect when something goes awry and direct the sympathetic nervous system to activate (fight or flight) or the parasympathetic nervous system, as last resource, to deactivate (go on "red alert," conserve energy by shutting down, and decreasing breathing and heart rate).

These two forms of dysregulation, HYPERAROUSAL and HYPOAROUSAL, are evolution's design to keep us safe. If these systems work well, they respond as necessary to the immediate threat or danger. When the threat is resolved, we move back to the WOT.

Depending on our experiences, our history of trauma, our early caregiving relationships, and our unique genetic makeup, the ability to resolve the sense of threat can be strong or weak. We can return with ease within a few moments or we can spend most of our lives dysregulated.

EXERCISE:

Let's review what you have learned so far. Place the appropriate word from this list by the scenario described below. Hyperaroused; Hypoaroused; Regulated.

1. Lucia is in traffic that has come to a standstill. She's sitting in her car, looking out the window, somewhat spaced out. When she looks up, there is a wide space between her and the car in front. Lucia is _____.

2. Lucia notices the space and accelerates to catch up with traffic. Suddenly, the car in front of its brakes. Lucia sees the red lights and reflexively slams on her brakes, stopping just in time. Her heart rate increases some. Lucia is _____.

3. After Lucia recognizes everything is okay, her heart rate returns to normal, and she continues to drive to work, paying attention to the road and thinking about her unfolding day. Lucia is _____.

4. A few days later, Lucia is again driving to work. Traffic is normal until it stops unexpectedly and Lucia crashes into the back of the car in front. To prevent the crash, Lucia's legs act quickly and put on the brakes but she can't stop the crash. After a while, she realizes her heart is racing, her breathing has quickened, and her legs and arms are shaking. Lucia is _____.

5. Lucia tries to get herself together and goes to work. When she gets there, she has some trouble concentrating. She tries to focus on her work but really can't. She feels sleepy. She has a thought that she needs to drive her slightly damaged car home and then spaces out. Lucia is _____.

EXERCISE: YOUR OWN RESPONSES

Take a moment to notice when you feel regulated. You might be feeling regulated right now or can remember a time when you did. What are you noticing in your body now or in the memory? Write three key phrases down.

_____   _____   _____

These are your indicators when you are regulated.

Now, take a moment and consider when you might have felt hyperaroused, the top band of the WOT dysregulation diagram. Write down the actual situation here:

_____

_____

What do you remember your body feeling? Write three words here:

_____   _____   _____

These are your indicators when you are hyperaroused.

Finally, take a moment and consider when you might have felt hypoaroused, the bottom band of the WOT dysregulation diagram. Write down the situation here:

_____

_____

What do you remember your body feeling? Write three words here:

_____   _____   _____

These are indicators of hypoarousal for you.

Take the time as you go through your everyday life to notice these different somatic states. The more you notice your own, the more you can be regulated when you work with clients. In so doing, you will be more able to regulate your clients and help them learn to regulate themselves.

[Please see Case Example on the next page.]

CASE EXAMPLE

Working with Hyperarousal
By Kathy Smith, MFT

Elena is a client with a complex trauma history referred by her primary doctor for PTSD treatment. During the first several sessions, she came in highly agitated and dysregulated.

Elena: Oh, I'm so upset . . .there was so much traffic on the way to your office . . . and then parking…

Therapist: I can see it was very stressful getting here. Let's see if we can slow things down a bit.

Elena: There's so many cars and I get nervous driving. . .

Therapist: Yes, (slowly) and you're here now and I'm here with you. Can you feel your feet on the floor? Just notice where your feet make contact with the floor. (I point to where my shoes are touching the rug. I want to orient Elena to somatic sensation). Can you feel your feet on the ground?

Elena: Yes.

Therapist: I'm going to move in a little closer. (I've already established in a previous session that Elena finds it helpful to have me physically closer to her. I'm using my own nervous system to help Elena regulate her sympathetic activation). So I'm here with you, Elena, just feel your feet and if you'd like you can close your eyes.

Elena: (Closes her eyes and takes a breath.) OK, I feel them.

Therapist: What else do you feel in your body right now?

Elena: I'm shaking . . I feel shaking in my arms and all over.

Therapist: So, just let that shaking be there . . .Just notice it . . . I'm here with you . . . It's OK to just let that happen . . . (some more breaths) . . . And what are you noticing now in your body?

Elena: It's less.

Therapist: There's less shaking?

Elena: Yes.

Therapist: So just notice that. Just feel the shaking slowing down . . . Looks like your breathing is slowing down, too.

Elena: Yes.

Therapist: (Speaking slowly and calmly.) So just notice that – your breathing is a little slower and deeper. (Continuing to orient client to somatic sensation). It looks like things are settling down inside of you. Is that right?

Elena: (Nods.)

Therapist: So just feel the settling. . . (I'm breathing slowly and audibly with the client).

Elena: (Smiles)

Therapist: Looks like this feels good.

Elena: Yes.

Therapist: Sometimes people will put one hand on their heart and the other on their abdomen. If you'd like, you can open your eyes and watch how I'm doing it right now.

Elena: (Opens her eyes and then places her hands similarly).

Therapist: Yes, like that. And, if you'd like, you can close your eyes again or keep them open, whatever is helpful. So just keep breathing nice and easily and feel your hands on your chest and your abdomen right now.

Elena: That feels good. (Smiles again)

Therapist: Yes, I'm doing it with you and it does feel good. So just let your body respond to the placement of your hands and the slow breath and notice what you feel emotionally right now.

Elena: I feel safe.

Therapist: So just let yourself feel safe right now. Just soak in that safe feeling.

---

2. Mindfulness as tool for regulation

◊ Mindfulness in somatic-based therapies is for the express purpose of observation of internal experience. The goal is not progressive relaxation or to free the brain from suffering.

◊ Mindfulness is the single biggest tool you will use both for regulating clients in dysregulated states and for working somatically when clients are regulated.

◊ Mindfulness in service of restoring regulation looks like this:
   a. Taking the time to slow down.
   b. Observing precisely what is happening in the body.
   c. Looking for somatic signs of dysregulation as the client experiences it.

Consider the following questions in light of your own experience or what your client might be experiencing:

What is your breathing like – shallow, rapid, very slow, normal?

How is your heart rate? – racing, very slow, normal?

Are your thoughts racing?

Are you scanning the environment?

What kind of energy is in your arms, legs?

Are you sweating? Is any part of your body shaking?

What is your internal temperature like – hot, cold, flushed, regular?

What is happening in your chest? Tight, open, collapsed, no feeling?

What is happening with your face? Twitching, tense, lip quivering?

Do you feel "out of your body"?

Do you feel like you are not quite "here"?

Do you feel numb?

What is your body stance like: upright, collapsed, rigid?

What is happening with your senses? What do you hear, see, smell?

What is happening in your stomach? Tight, nauseous, open?

What does the therapist do?

    a. NOTICE and ASK what is happening with the client?

    b. What is happening with you now? When you close your eyes and go inside, tell me exactly what you are noticing?

OR

    c. I notice your chin is quivering. Do you notice that? Can you hear my voice? Are you aware of being here with me?

Once you and the client begin working in the somatic realm, once you are working mindfully with the present-moment somatic state of the client, you are at that precise moment beginning to regulate the client.

Mindfulness by itself is a regulator. It offers dual awareness: observing and experiencing at the same time; being in contact with self and with another at the same time.

EXERCISE:

Place hypoaroused, hyperaroused, or regulated next to each statement. What state is the client most likely in?

1. A client's eyes seem glassy and vacant. _____

2. A client is holding their breath. _____

3. A client is speaking very fast. _____

4. A client's foot is tapping rapidly. _____

5. A client's gaze is even and calm. _____

6. A client's face is flushed. _____

7. A client's voice cadence is steady and regular. _____

8. A client's face is pale. _____

9. A client's lip is quivering. _____

10. A client's shoulders and chest are collapsed. _____

Think of your own clients: Write three somatic descriptors of a client whom you think is often hypoaroused:

_____   _____   _____

Write three somatic descriptors of a client whom you think is often hyperaroused:

_____   _____   _____

3. Resourcing

Survival Resources

Hyperaroused and hypoaroused states are the body's SURVIVAL resources for dealing with life's threats, dangers, and stresses. All dysregulated reactions stem from a person's largely unconscious wisdom to survive. Even if they are not the most healthy behaviors, such as anger outbursts, or drinking to blackout, they are an attempt to manage what feels intolerable and to psychically stay alive.

It is vital that therapists view these behaviors as survival resources, as having their own wisdom. To see these survival resources as resistance or avoidance works against the client's internal capacity to heal in their own time and way.

Examples of Survival Resources:

1. Cutting, self-harm
2. Depression, anxiety, self-blame
3. Addictions
4. Dissociative states, alters
5. High-risk behaviors such as extreme sports (possibly)
6. Isolation
7. Fast speech, interrupting
8. Avoiding eye contact
9. Shame
10. Self-doubt
11. Risk-averse behaviors
12. Grasping for connection/attachment
13. Rigid or overloose boundaries
14. Overachievement/Overproductiveness

Take a moment and consider two of your clients. For each one, name three survival resources:

1. Initials: ____ _____   _____   _____

2. Initials: ____ _____   _____   _____

Take a moment and consider yourself. Name three survival resources you use now or have used in the past:

_____   _____   _____

We want our clients to notice where they are in the Window of Tolerance. Are they regulated? Hyperaroused? Hypoaroused?

Using mindfulness, we can track where clients are in the WOT and begin to teach them to track themselves. If you notice a client is dysregulated, resourcing helps bring them back into the WOT.

Creative Resources

Resources that bring us back into the WOT are called CREATIVE resources and, in general, enable us to live safely and happily.

Examples:

1. Mindfulness
2. Self-acceptance
3. Compassion and self-compassion
4. Meditation
5. Exercise
6. Nature
7. Spiritual practice
8. Friendship
9. Intimate, securely-attached relationship
10. Therapy
11. Massage
12. Correctly prescribed, effective psychotropic medications
13. Creativity
14. Love
15. Humor and laughter
16. Play
17. Sensuality and sexuality
18. Psychoeducation
19. Unique images, spirit guides, important childhood figures
20. Somatic Resources *

*Somatic resources is the most important and effective category of creative resources to use in the room with the client or for the client to use on a moment-by-moment basis outside of therapy. (The teaching of somatic resources was initially developed by Sensorimotor Psychotherapy Institute).

Using mindfulness helps you and the client notice what is happening somatically as they becomes dysregulated. Once you identify if the client is hyperaroused or hypoaroused, you can use specific, concrete body-based interventions to help them regulate. You can observe or ask your client to tell you what is happening in their body. Below are techniques for managing each state of dysregulation.

For Hyperarousal:

1. Focus on calming the nervous system.

2. Focus on exhalation. Let out more breath than is brought in. Breathe in 2-3 counts; breathe out 3-4 counts.

3. Bring person into present by focusing on their five senses. What do they see, hear, taste, physically feel, smell? Bring the person's awareness to what they notice in the present of each sense, e.g., "Name all the green things in the room"; "Pay close attention and tell me what you hear in this room or from the outside."

4. Use active somatic resources directed toward calming the SNS:
   a. Right hand under left armpit with left hand on right shoulder. This resource helps the person feel the container of their body.
   b. Hand on forehead, other hand on chest: Direct them to feel the flow of energy, possible change in temperature and pace of heartbeat.
   c. Hand on heart, other hand on belly: Direct them to feel the taking in of breath and the exhaling of breath and to feel the warmth and comfort of their hands on their body.
   d. Tapping different parts of the body, such as butterfly tap or moving throughout the body tapping different parts.
   e. Squeeze different muscle groups.

For Hypoarousal:

1. Focus on enlivening/oxygenating the nervous system.

2. Focus on inhalation. Breathe in 3-4 counts, breathe out 2-3.

3. Direct person to make eye contact if they can. Say in calm but energetic voice: "Let's get you back into your body." Have the person flex their feet, hands, quadriceps, upper forearm muscles, and press their palms against each other.

4. Direct person to stand up and feel the ground, feel each foot as it hits ground, and feel the ground beneath their feet.

5. Have client do a set of pushups against the wall or downward-facing dog pose.

6. Bring humor and playfulness: Toss balls or pillows, do tug of war, or play with a slinky.

7. Direct person to straighten their spine, and feel the energy moving up through the top of their head.

Special, Powerful Category of Somatic Resources:

Instinctive, unconscious soothing movements and gestures are particularly effective. These include: stroking hair; caressing fingers, arms, hands, thighs; flexing feet, hands; deep breathing and sighing; hand on heart; particular movement of the face and movement of body in space. Notice and encourage repetition of the movement/gesture.

Attachment/Somatic Resource for Dysregulation

Hyperarousal: "Your body is taking care of you. It is sensing threat or danger and therefore trying to protect you. Let yourself hear my calm voice here with you now in the present. Here in the present, you and I together, there is no threat."

Hypoarousal: "Try looking at me, tell me what you notice about me. Can you hear my voice? Are you aware of being in the room with me? Bring your awareness to the space between us, to your connection with me in this moment, to the memory of feeling safe with me, what that feels like in your body right here, right now." Depending on your (therapist) level of comfort, offer touch – "Can you feel my hand?"

All of these suggestions for helping your client return to the Window of Tolerance would be enhanced by the use of basic somatic skills. Please read Chapters 13 – 18: Neuroscience and Theory of Tracking; Tracking and Contacting; Slowing; Supporting the Wisdom of Defenses; Deepening One and Two; Special Consideration: Use of Touch.

Chapter 6

Introduction to Trauma Treatments: EMDR and Sensorimotor Psychotherapy

---

Somatic, emotional and cognitive responses to discrete or developmental trauma are often not integrated. Why? As we know, when trauma occurs, the brainstem initiates a physical response which then gets transmitted to the limbic system to send out a full body alarm (amygdala). Sympathetic or dorsal vagal parasympathetic responses include suppressing the hippocampus' ability to appraise whether escape is possible or the trauma is real in the present.

If the incident sets up an internal belief that one is going to die, those responses continue in a loop and get stored in non-integrated systems. The communication between the amygdala and the hippocampus may be faulty or impaired. This means lack of bilateral brain integration. As a result, the hippocampus cannot bring in left-brain functioning which can take the experience and make it a story of the past. By making the event a story of the past rather than the present, the left brain offers meaning to the event and stops the stuck cycle.

This chapter is intended solely as a brief introduction to trauma treatments. For more information about trauma literature and trainings, please consult the "Bibliography" and "Resources" sections in the Appendix.

Eye-Movement Desensitization and Reprocessing (EMDR)

EMDR functions on the premise of integrating these aspects of the left and right brains by using bilateral stimulation. It assumes that crossing the midline of the brain (corpus callosum) will facilitate this integration. It is unclear what makes EMDR work. It could be the above or could be dual awareness: As the bilateral stimulation is happening, the person focuses on both the traumatic experience and all the somatic, emotional, and cognitive disturbances it evokes while, at the same time, bringing attention to the tapping, listening or eye movements.

A key component of unresolved trauma, particularly discrete trauma, is a stuck negative core belief. EMDR directly targets that belief.

Whenever you are working with any kind of trauma, it is crucial that you identify a resource for safety if the person moves too far out of the Window of Tolerance. This is a lesson from past therapies gone awry: Do not retraumatize the person.

Sensorimotor Psychotherapy

Sensorimotor Psychotherapy has a different approach to the same neuroscience: sequencing and completion. It focuses much more on what is held in the body. Sensorimotor works directly with the physiological responses to trauma: fight, flight, submit, and freeze. These responses are activated during a trauma and either completed or not completed. If a person feels their life is endangered and there is no escape through the active responses of fight or flight, they will respond with the passive responses of submit or freeze. When submitting or freezing, the flight/fight responses are still held in the nervous system. The goal is to change the passive responses of submit and freeze to the held active responses of flight/fight which can then be completed.

Completion enables the held flight/fight responses to complete themselves through micromovements—small and large gestures of fight or flight until there is a nervous system settling. This is called sequencing as the therapist guides the client through the sequence of responses and held responses to the event through to the settling. There are often many waves of this sequencing.

Sequencing utilizes the WOT more precisely than EMDR. The therapist is working with the client within a range just outside the WOT where the client is still aware of the present. As the client is working, the therapist will softly resource them through the sequencing or more assertively resource the client if they are too far out of the WOT.

In both EMDR and Sensorimotor, the therapist works with the client to establish a viable resource that has particular meaning to that client. In EMDR, the resource is usually an image with attendant positive sensory memories; in Sensorimotor, the resource is an image/experience of something normal/good that was happening before the incident accompanied by a somatic resource.

Stages of Trauma Recovery
By Janina Fisher, Ph.D., © 2000[*]

STAGE I: Safety and Stabilization: Overcoming Dysregulation

At this stage, the role of the therapist is to teach the client how to take charge of the treatment, rather than helplessly responding to a dysregulated mind and body. In order to become actively involved in the work of safety and stabilization, the client must first be taught to comprehend the effects of trauma: to become familiar with the common symptoms of trauma, de-code cause-effect relationships between traumatic reminders and triggered experience, and understand the meaning of autonomic dysregulation, intrusive affects and distorted cognitive schemas. The achievement of safety and stability rests on accomplishing the following tasks:

- Establishment of **bodily safety**: e.g., abstinence from self-injury, sobriety, attention to basic self-care, and attention to bodily health.

---

[*] From: Herman, J. (1992). *Trauma and Recovery*. New York: Basic Books.

- Establishment of a **safe environment:** e.g., a secure living situation, non-abusive relationships, a job and/or regular income, adequate supports.
- Establishment of **emotional stability**: e.g., ability to calm the body, regulate affect, self-soothe, set healthy boundaries, and manage depressive and post-traumatic symptoms triggered by mundane events.

The goal of this stage is to create **a safe and stable "life in the here-and-now"** which will allow the client to safely **remember** the trauma, rather than **re-live** it.

STAGE II: Processing the Traumatic Memories

The goal of this stage is the **integration of traumatic memories**, feelings, and cognitions into a personal narrative, creating new meaning for the client and a clearer sense of self. Because most survivors have few or incomplete memories and little sense of the context in which the trauma occurred, processing is much like putting together a large jigsaw puzzle. In order to metabolize (not just verbalize) the trauma, the client may need to make use of EMDR, hypnotherapy, or mind-body therapies at this stage. Throughout, s/he must also be attentive to pacing so as not to become either "stuck" in avoidance of the pain or overwhelmed by memories and flashbacks. Since "remembering is not recovering," it is only necessary to find ways of **coming to terms with the traumatic past**, rather than seeking to uncover all of its details.

STAGE III: Integration and Moving On

The client can now begin to work on decreasing the sense of shame and alienation, on developing a greater capacity for healthy intimacy, and on taking up personal and professional goals that reflect how s/he has made meaning out of having survived and healed from traumatic abuse. As the survivor's life becomes reconsolidated around a **healthy present and a healed self**, the trauma becomes increasingly farther away, part of an integrated understanding of self but no longer a daily focus.

Part II
Attachment Through a Somatic Lens

Chapter 7

Attachment History: Bowlby, Ainsworth, Main, and the Strange Situation

A s we move from learning about affect regulation into attachment, it is important to recognize one key overriding concept: The essence of attachment is co-
regulation or other-regulation. When we discuss working with affect regulation
with clients, we are dealing with their intrapersonal experience in the moment. As we help
regulate them, we are other-regulating them and, from this, they can learn to self-regulate.

Current attachment theory details the consequences over a lifetime of inadequate
co- or other-regulation of the infant/child by caregivers. The qualities of this inadequacy
form the basis for the kinds of insecure attachment that can develop.

As most therapists know, the history of attachment began with John Bowlby, a Brit-
ish psychoanalyst who trained with Melanie Klein. His life and professional experiences,
however, led him to differ significantly from traditional psychoanalysis. Most analysts
of the time linked attachment to the infant's need for food. Bowlby, by contrast, saw the
infant in its real-world environment where the mother or caregiver's attention and emotional approach was the basis of a successful attachment.

His views stemmed from his work and research. Before, during and after World War
II, he worked in clinics with delinquent children, children separated from parents in Lon-
don to protect them from bombing raids, the Kinder Transport of Jewish children during
the Holocaust, and group nurseries of children whose mothers worked during the war.

He wrote in a commissioned monograph by the United Nations in 1951, "The infant and young child should experience a warm, intensive, and continuous relationship with his/her mother (or permanent mother substitute) in which both find satisfaction and enjoyment." (http://en.wikipedia.org/wiki/John_Bowlby). He was also influenced by the work of Harry Harlow who proved with his cloth monkey/metal monkey experiments that comfort and softness mattered more in infant development than food.

Heredity and genetics as well as later life experiences were a factor, Bowlby theorized, but the early caregiving environment was crucial. Two aspects were critical:

- Death of mother/early separation
- Emotional attitude of mother

Bowlby's understanding of these two factors, seen through the lens of real world experiences, led to the development of his attachment theory. (The word, "attachment," stemmed from Konrad Lorenz' study of the imprinting of ducklings.) His writing, published through the World Health Organization in the early 1950's, had profound effects on the treatment of children in child development clinics, hospitals, and orphanages.

Because his views differed radically from psychoanalysis, he was scorned by that community and needed to find a way to prove his theory empirically. He found a partner in Mary Ainsworth whose work studying parenting behaviors with children and families in Uganda led eventually to "The Strange Situation," the foundational assessment tool.

Through their work and that of other attachment theorists, it is now widely-believed that attachment behaviors are evolutionarily hard-wired through infants' limbic systems for the purpose of feeding but also for psychological and physical survival and development.

Below is a list of notable attachment behaviors:

- Sucking
- Clinging
- Following
- Crying
- Smiling

- Cooing
- Babbling

As caregivers with their own wired-in attachment behaviors attune to the infant, the infant receives necessary comfort, protection, and a feeling of security. Bowlby and Ainsworth's definition of attachment is the following: "Use of a preferred person as a secure base from which to explore…and as a haven of safety and comfort when needed." They continue with this definition — Attachment Security: "Confidence that the secure base person will 'always be there for me', available, responsive and able to help or save me." (Both quotes are taken from YouTube Video, "Strange Situation Experiment.mp4", by April Mayhem.)

"The Strange Situation," Mary Ainsworth's research tool with 12-month-old infants and their primary caregivers, led to the theorizing and verification of three categories of attachment style.

- Secure
- Insecure: Anxious/Ambivalent (resistant)
- Insecure: Anxious/Avoidant

Mary Main, a colleague of Ainsworth, later added a third category of insecure attachment:

- Insecure: Disorganized/Disoriented

Later research differentiated child attachment from adult attachment and different terminology was developed for insecure attachment. For the purposes of this workbook, we will use the following terms to describe adult attachment: Secure; Preoccupied; Avoidant or Dismissing; Disorganized.

As I noted in the introduction to this section, attachment is primarily about the adequate regulation of an infant's nervous system by the caregiver. This understanding of attachment developed after the widespread use of the concept and word, "style." Although the language of "styles" is still used effectively, neuroscience advances in the 1990s offered a more specific physiological understanding: Attachment strategies are differing responses prompted by attempts to regulate the nervous system during stressful interpersonal situations. From this view, no one person has any one style or is always in that state of mind.

The Strange Situation

Below is a description of the Strange Situation's focus, methodology, and assessments. After reading this section, you might want to take a look at the YouTube video, "Strange Situation Experiment," mp4, by April Mayhem. The experiment, as originally structured, places a 12-month-old infant with their primary caregiver in a research playroom. Information about the Strange Situation below is taken from http://en.wikipedia.org/wiki/Strange_situation.

The experiment has nine steps although it is often conducted in modified fashion using fewer steps or only one episode of separation and reunion. These steps are:

- Parent and infant are introduced to the experimental room.
- Parent and infant are alone. Parent does not participate while infant explores.
- Stranger enters, converses with parent, then approaches infant. Parent leaves inconspicuously.
- First separation episode: Stranger's behavior is geared to that of infant.
- First reunion episode: Parent returns. Stranger leaves. Parent greets and comforts infant, then leaves again.
- Second separation episode: Infant is alone.
- Continuation of second separation episode: Stranger enters and gears behavior to that of infant.
- Second reunion episode: Parent enters, greets infant, and picks up infant. Stranger leaves inconspicuously.

The focus of the experiment is to observe the following in the 12-month-olds:

- The amount of play or exploration the child engages in throughout the observation.
- The child's reaction to caregiver's departure.
- Stranger anxiety in response to the stranger.
- The child's reunion behavior with its caregiver.

The following behaviors indicate a Secure infant attachment:

- Explores freely when mother is present.
- Engages with stranger when mother is in room.
- Visibly upset when caregiver leaves the room.
- Happy to see caregiver return.

Etiology of level of security: Timely, attuned care of child with contingent communication, focused on child's needs but includes development of stress tolerance.

The following behaviors indicate a Preoccupied (Anxious) infant attachment:

- Anxious in regard to exploration and the stranger even with caregiver present.
- Very distressed when caregiver leaves.
- When caregiver returns, shows ambivalence, wants to be close but also resists, maybe doing things like hitting mother and pulling away while still in mother's arms.

Etiology of level of security: May stem from inconsistent responses from caregiver, more reflective of mother's needs: Infant does not feel secure that its needs will be attended to in a timely, attuned way.

The following behaviors indicate an Avoidant (Dismissing) Infant attachment:

- Ignores or avoids caregiver when she is present and when she returns.
- May run away from caregiver and not cling when she picks him up upon return.
- Strangers and caregivers may be treated the same with little emotional range.

Etiology of level of security: Stems from a caregiving style that is more disengaged, harsh, or dismissing: Infant's emotional needs are not met and infant has given up, believing unconsciously that communication will not help.

The following behaviors indicate a Disorganized infant attachment:

- Shows contradictory behavior such as crying during separation but avoiding caregiver upon return.
- May move toward mother, then move away.
- May do stereotyped behaviors such as rocking, hitting self, flapping arms.

Etiology of level of security: Stems from caregiver's unresolved trauma or grief that causes disorganized responses in child, or abuse by caregiver: Infant is left needing caregiver but afraid of her at the same time.

(Note: Information from this chapter was taken from various sources including *Becoming Attached* (Karen, 1999), *Being a Brain-Wise Therapist* (Badenoch, 2008) and several common-use online sites such as Wikipedia.)

ATTACHMENT LEARNING POINTS EXERCISE:

1. What is the main difference between Freud's and the psychoanalytic community's early theory about the need for attachment and Bowlby's theory?

   _____

2. What are the two environmental factors Bowlby thought most influenced attachment? (Choose two)
   a. Race
   b. Birth order
   c. Emotional attitude of mother/caregiver
   d. Early separation from or death of mother/caregiver

      e. Poverty

      f. Presence of extended family

3. Name five biologically-encoded infant attachment behaviors:

      a. _____ b. _____ c. _____

      d. _____ e. _____

4. Bowlby was influenced by Konrad Lorenz and his study of _____ _____.

5. Name the three different attachment styles Mary Ainsworth delineated in her Strange Situation experiment and the last one added by Mary Main. Next to each style, identify the "reunion" behavior the infant demonstrates:

      a. _____   _____

      b. _____   _____

      c. _____   _____

      d. _____   _____

Chapter 8

Four Attachment Styles Charts

R ead the following charts regarding different attachment styles. Exercises at the end of the charts will cement your learning.

NOTE: The charts are comprehensive and include information that is covered in later chapters. If you do not understand a term, please consult the Glossary in the Appendix. If you do not understand a neuroscience concept, please read Chapters 9 and 10. The ideas reflected in these charts are an integration of the reading and thinking I have done about attachment. Please see the Bibliography for specific sources.

This chapter contains a compilation of information about the identified four styles of attachment: one secure and three insecure styles. My intention is to provide a sense of how attachment may play out across the life span, in relationships and work, in assessment situations, and in therapy, and offers brief suggestions for treatment interventions. As we will discuss later in a new model of attachment, people have attachment tendencies or strategies rather than styles and can shift amongst the different categories depending on a number of factors. Discrete categorization is important for the facilitation of therapist learning but flexible application will be needed in actual clinical practice.

SECURE ATTACHMENT: Primary System

TERMINOLOGY: Birth – 2 years = secure; 2 years (Rapprochement) – adolescence = secure; Adult = secure, free, autonomous, earned or learned secure attachment.

STRANGE SITUATION: Able to play with or without mother before mother leaves the room; becomes gradually upset about mother's absence; on mother's return, is easily soothed and quickly returns to play.

18 MONTHS TO 36 MONTHS: (Rapprochement) Able to move between contact with mother and being engaged elsewhere; trusting they can return to mother and mother will be there (object constancy and secure base); seeks comfort and accepts soothing when distressed; uses language and body to express broad range of feelings; engages in and accepts repair when there is misattunement.

ADOLESCENCE: Able to successfully shift focus to peer group but can rely on parents when threatened or stressed; can experiment and take risks but usually exercises good judgment; stays engaged with family, initiates and accepts repair; able to connect with friends; experiences disappointments and failures with sense of self intact, using comfort and support of both friends and family.

ADULTHOOD: Able to work and play in balance; seeks comfort from a significant other or others when threatened or stressed and able to use soothing or to self-soothe (internalized sense of secure base); initiates and accepts efforts of repair; seeks closeness and contact while able to be securely independent; mostly operates in present moment rather than in reaction to past (ample Window of Tolerance).

ADULT ATTACHMENT INTERVIEW: Coherent narrative which embraces the difficulties as well as happiness of childhood, expressed with sense of fluidity, ease, self-awareness and self-acceptance; spoken narrative congruent with body language, facial expression, and energy.

ETIOLOGY/NEUROSCIENCE: Uses primary attachment system – seeks proximity with available and responsive other when dysregulated; social engagement system generally operating well through Ventral Vagus Nerve of Autonomic Nervous System; regulation restored easily due to vertical right brain integration and horizontal left brain-right brain integration.

WHAT WE SEE IN THERAPY: Comes to therapy for issues of grief, transitions, adjustment to difficult circumstances, managing parts of identity not supported by outside world; able to have reasonable amount of trust with therapist, expresses feelings and thoughts freely; connection feels generally present; able to use therapist interventions; can voice disconnections with therapist, or, if not, can acknowledge it when therapist names it, and can accept repair; good eye contact; body, narrative congruent; adult has reasonable outline of coherent narrative; adolescent sees parents fairly accurately, open and able to begin connecting dots.

COUNTERTRANSFERENCE: Generally feel connected to client; feel competent, warm, loving; may have strong feelings of connection and hard to separate self from client pain.

THERAPEUTIC INTERVENTIONS: Any theory or intervention will have some effectiveness; Rogerian, empathic, body-oriented therapies easily accepted and integrated.

PREOCCUPIED ATTACHMENT: "Can Feel But Not Deal"

TERMINOLOGY: Birth – 2 years = anxious-resistant; 2 years (Rapprochement) – adolescence = anxious-ambivalent; Adult = Preoccupied.

STRANGE SITUATION: Difficulty focusing on play; stays engaged with mother before she leaves; very distressed upon return; has difficulty being comforted (co-regulated), alternating between crying, expressing anger like batting things away; hard to get back to play.

18 MONTHS TO 36 MONTHS: (Rapprochement) Separation anxiety continues for long time; fearful of leaving mother and engaging in play; demonstrates clingy, unsoothable energy; sense of joy muted by fear; emotional range more characterized by overwhelm, hyperarousal; comfort from mother may take a long time to be effective; fearful of taking risks, exploring; object constancy and secure base are not effectively established.

ADOLESCENCE: Able to engage in school and peer groups but with some anxiety, lack of self-confidence; highly reactive to real or perceived slights; tendency to have intense, conflictual relationships; tries to use friends and family for comfort but absorbing soothing is difficult; dysregulation common with narrowed WOT; disappointments and failures reinforce low self-esteem; susceptible to addictions, self-harming behaviors without intervention of good-enough other who is steady, secure, available and non-intrusive.

ADULTHOOD: Work performance may be affected by interpersonal difficulty at work and preoccupation with interpersonal issues; comfort and support may be available but person has hard time feeling soothed, satisfied with the support that is available; reactive to real or perceived slights; when stressed, may overwhelm support system with obsessive need for reassurance, constantly perseverating on stressful interactions; poor boundaries; tendency toward hyperarousal; exhibits over-dependency; mostly operating in reaction to recent or distant past (narrowed WOT).

ADULT ATTACHMENT INTERVIEW: Narrative mixes past experiences with present experiences as if they are currently happening; telling story can provoke overwhelm of emotion and body reactions; wealth of detail, sense of tangentiality, looping, hyperarousal during the telling.

ETIOLOGY/NEUROSCIENCE: Uses secondary attachment system: hyperactivating – seeks proximity with available and responsive other when dysregulated but cannot receive the nourishment that is available (parenting was inconsistent, serving moment to moment needs of parent more than child); Ventral Vagus Nerve perceives danger, deactivates social engagement system of attachment and prompts limbic system sympathetic activation of flight and fight; lack of vertical right-brain and horizontal left-right brain integration.

WHAT WE SEE IN THERAPY: Presenting problems: depression, anxiety, loneliness, low-self-esteem, relationship difficulties, feeling rejected; loose boundaries re: therapy—pushes for more time, frequent calls or emails; very engaged with relationship, sometimes with idealization, sometimes with disappointment/anger/devaluation; can move rapidly between hyperarousal and hypoarousal; resents framework of therapy because client wants more of a relationship; usually a ready trust with therapist; focused on highly-detailed storytelling about ways they have been hurt or mistreated or what's wrong with them, self-castigation; can accept empathy, repair with a bit of time.

COUNTERTRANSFERENCE: Therapist can feel flattered by client's attachment/idealization or flattened by devaluation; can feel very attached and empathic but overwhelmed, smothered, exhausted and burned out; may feel anxious/not good enough when client does not appear to be doing better, continues to have trouble with regulation.

THERAPEUTIC INTERVENTIONS: Meet client with empathy for suffering; immediately teach and practice regulation, WOT, mindfulness, resourcing; seek life stability if unstable before doing depth somatic work; keep countertransference in check by setting clear boundaries in a loving way; work on actively developing object constancy.

AVOIDANT/DISMISSING ATTACHMENT: "Can Deal But Not Feel"

TERMINOLOGY: Birth – 2 years = anxious-avoidant; 2 years (Rapprochement) – adolescence = avoidant; Adult = dismissing.

STRANGE SITUATION: Shows little outward emotional response to mother's departure or return; will engage in play easily; does not particularly show a preference for mother over stranger; may respond to mother's efforts to comfort by physically pulling or pushing away.

18 MONTHS TO 36 MONTHS: (Rapprochement) Can be very engaged with things, toys, self-play; will generally not seek support from parent except under extremely stressful circumstances; expression of feeling range limited; may appear withdrawn or shy around other children or adults; relationship with parents marked by support for independence, disapproval of need for comfort, crying, etc.

ADOLESCENCE: Can function well in world of work or school; can be high-achiever; may tend to be somewhat of a loner but with some buddies; feeling outside the group may cause the person to isolate or to retreat into use of substances that can make social engagement easier; susceptible to depression or overfocus on schoolwork; relationship with parents not close but reliable; high expectations by parents; stress may cause somatic symptoms as there are few outlets for unacknowledged emotion.

ADULTHOOD: High-functioning and successful at work; may seek relationship, get married, but quality of intimacy is limited; works from a one-person psychology rather than from the perspective of relationship; partners and sometimes, children or co-workers, reflect feelings of disconnection and loneliness which are often a surprise; processes stress internally with little consciousness or self-awareness; does not view other people as sources of comfort; narrowed WOT with tendency toward hypoarousal in terms of relationship.

ADULT ATTACHMENT INTERVIEW: Narrative is marked by a paucity of detail, tendency to paint picture of happy childhood without a sense of emotional texture; when asked to describe relationship with parents, will tend to discuss things such as a parent's skills, abilities, characteristics other than emotional qualities or relationship qualities; facial expression and body can convey distance or shutdown.

ETIOLOGY/NEUROSCIENCE: Uses secondary attachment system – deactivating: shuts off need for connection/comfort due to "hidden layer" formed by early caregiving experiences when seeking proximity was dysregulating: when proximity was sought, caregiver was physically available but provided negative, shaming, harsh response; ANS Dorsal Vagal Nerve deactivates social engagement system because contact and attachment represent threat to self/life; limited right brain vertical integration and limited horizontal integration; mostly responding to past "hidden layers" with respect to relationships, own need for comfort/attachment.

WHAT WE SEE IN THERAPY: Comes to therapy for issues related to rejection, being left by partners, depression, sense of isolation, something missing, stress of workaholism or addictions, lack of meaning; can often talk in detail about work and concrete things; emotional range can be limited; storytelling without much internal focus; fear of judgment and feelings of shame as they reveal more; therapist may be overvalued as an expert or the relationship with therapist might be devalued as relationships are generally devalued; eye contact can be difficult; processing can cause resentment or anxiety; body language can show guardedness and distance.

COUNTERTRANSFERENCE: May feel disconnected, distanced, like you are not doing a good job; may feel the client is not engaged/committed; may fear triggering feelings of vulnerability or shame; may feel angry if client cancels sessions or seems to devalue the relationship.

THERAPEUTIC INTERVENTIONS: Meet client's most immediate presenting need rather than too much empathy; use less "warm and fuzzy" language; start with psycho-education in order to name and reduce shame; get client's buy-in prior to doing mindfulness/somatics; track client responses carefully for shame or uncomfortable vulnerability; let client feel in control of session and what happens; keep countertransference in check so that you can stay engaged; use humor/playfulness.

DISORGANIZED ATTACHMENT: "Fright Without Solution" *

TERMINOLOGY: Birth – 2 years = disorganized/disoriented; 2 years (Rapprochement) – adolescence = disorganized/disoriented; Adult = unresolved.

STRANGE SITUATION: Shows confused and contradictory responses to mother in the room and when she returns from separation; may move toward and then back from mother; may exhibit repetitive behaviors like waving hands without purpose; may freeze up; may open and closed eyes repeatedly, look at mother, then away and back.

18 MONTHS TO 36 MONTHS: (Rapprochement) Depending on severity of disorganization, behaviors are apt to fall generally in either an avoidant or a preoccupied tendency with pockets of disorganization prompted by fear or perceptions of interpersonal threat.

ADOLESCENCE: Depending on level of continuing exposure to parental threat/neglect, can learn critical academic skills and have some friendships; relationships can be marked by confusion and contradiction for both the person and their important others; symptoms of traumatic dysregulation may pop up in unexpected circumstances, leaving the person vulnerable, feeling unsafe, and unsure how to be in a given situation; relationships can be very intense and confusing; commonly demonstrates self-injurious behaviors, dissociation and extreme use of substances in attempts to cope with the anxiety/terror of internal experiences.

ADULTHOOD: Depending on severity, can have significant difficulty functioning in work and in relationships; highly reactive and sensitive to perception of external physical and emotional threat; functions frequently in fear, feeling of entrapment, internal collapse; may exhibit behaviors with serious life consequences such as suicide attempts, physical fights, high-risk behaviors; could chronically be on high-alert hypervigilance or intermittently dissociated and possibly in harm's way; less severely disorganized may only have episodic experiences and may generally function adequately with avoidant or preoccupied attachment strategies.

ADULT ATTACHMENT INTERVIEW: Narrative marked by memories of abuse or neglect that are not integrated and not clear; distortions in perceptions of other may be noticeable; story may be told in a state of hyperarousal or dissociation as they move into memories as if in present time; sense of fear and danger permeate the narrative counterbalanced by attempts to integrate feelings of love and caring for parents; rage and tearfulness intermix in narrative.

* Phrase by Main and Hesse, 1999

ETIOLOGY/NEUROSCIENCE: Caregiver was simultaneously the person who took care of child and also frightened child (caregiver may have been terrified or terrifying): proximity was necessary but frightening; caregiver may have had unresolved grief or trauma, been abusive or neglectful, severely and chronically depressed; home difficulties may be compounded by violence, lack of safety, daily threat in the neighborhood/community; may have been significant maternal separations or caregiver death during critical period of limbic development; frequent and/or chronic activation of the Autonomic Nervous System, particularly sympathetic-adrenal activation of fight/flight and dorsal vagal de-activation of freeze (dissociation, shame, submission); ventral vagal social engagement system allowing for attachment, rest, self-soothing and reception of comfort from others is frequently inhibited.

WHAT WE SEE IN THERAPY: Comes to therapy for issues related to overall life dysfunction; may have experiences of victimization and victimizing; may be court-ordered; depending on temperament, degree of life problems, and available resources, may have seen many therapists or been through many self-help programs; tends to be operating mostly in dysregulation coping with fear, rage, confusion, rejection, perhaps paranoia/suspiciousness; may feel compelled to stay dysregulated to feel safe.

COUNTERTRANSFERENCE: May feel overwhelmed, fearful for client safety, overinvolved, prone to erode boundaries, exhausted by reality of client needs, frustrated by client approach/avoidance, impaired functioning and life disorganization; may believe client needs are beyond therapist's capacities; may feel scared by client at times.

THERAPEUTIC INTERVENTIONS: Assess for safety in client's life and in therapy; establish safety plan if necessary; establish solid frame for therapy that addresses client need for consistency or more contact while taking care of self and boundaries; consider medication evaluation if appropriate; may need to collaborate closely with psychiatrist or adjunctive therapist, social worker; use intuition/right-brain to feel for presence of ANS dysregulation in therapy; use own nervous system to regulate client in session until client can begin to internalize and self-regulate; as client stabilizes, provide psychoeducation about what the client may be experiencing; slowly introduce trauma treatments with regulation as a base principle; attend to secondary attachment systems as they appear in therapy.

CHART EXERCISE:

Complete the following statements with the appropriate attachment style: (secure, preoccupied, avoidant/dismissing, disorganized) A given statement could be true of more than one style. I am using the word "style" but, as mentioned before and as you will read further in the workbook, a newer model of attachment uses the concept of a system that is activated at any particular moment and is therefore not fixed. Use of the word "tendency" or "strategy" may be more helpful.

1. In the Adult Attachment Interview, a person with this style tends to paint a glowing picture of their childhood. _____

2. A person with a _____ style might have difficulty making consistent eye contact.

3. Someone seems very connected in therapy but has a hard time keeping appointments. _____

4. In the Strange Situation, a _____ infant exhibits conflicting behavior such as moving towards its mother and then away.

5. A client seems to have a good understanding of what has happened in their life that has created problems and joys. _____

6. A person who seems _____ may have had a caregiver who was critical and harsh in attitude and behavior toward them while growing up.

7. A chronically depressed parent could be a causal factor in the development of a _____ style.

8. A client who is fearful of not being liked or being abandoned might have a _____ style.

9. A client seems able to balance work and play. _____

10. A client overworks and has difficulty asking for help. _____

11. You experience your client as very needy and it is hard for you to keep boundaries you set. _____

12. You like your client a lot but are not sure they feel connected to you. _____

13. An adolescent is frequently stressed but doesn't seem able to absorb the support and comfort that is available to her. _____

14. Safety issues dominate the therapy. _____

15. Shame and fear of judgment are constant experiences for this person. _____

16. A caregiver is inconsistent in their availability and attunement to their child. This is one factor in a potential _____ style.

17. This person may be more susceptible to anxiety. _____

18. This person may be more susceptible to depression. _____

19. A client seems to devalue relationships and their own needs. _____

20. You feel connected and sessions move smoothly. _____

21. This person may tend to use alcohol as their substance of choice. _____

22. This person may tend to use stimulants as their substance of choice. _____

23. You sometimes find yourself feeling bored in sessions. _____

24. You find yourself worrying a lot about this client in between sessions. _____

25. In the Strange Situation, this infant wants comfort from his mother when she returns, but can't accept it, clinging to her while being angry. _____

Chapter 9

Basic Neuroscience of Attachment

As we move further into the study of attachment, we begin to look at what is actually happening for the infant on a physiological, body-brain level. In the last chapter, I referred to attachment as essentially reflecting the quality of interpersonal regulation in early years that facilitated a person's later effective self-regulation.*

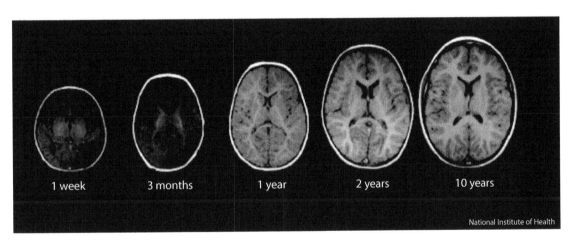

Let's take a look at the picture above from an article called, "The Deterministic Myth of 'The Early Years,'" by Helene Guldberg (www.spiked-online.com, July 16, 2013). Here we can see in a tangible way just how important those early years are.

The picture demonstrates the reality of child brain development. At two years, the size of the child's brain is more than ¾ the size of the 10-year-old brain. Look how much

---

* Note: Some information from this chapter comes from *The Neuroscience of Psychotherapy*, Louis Cozolino, 2002, and *The Science of the Art of Psychotherapy*, Allan N Schore, 2012.

development has already happened by 2 years! Given this, we can't afford to ignore the significance of the first few years in emotional and cognitive development. Some things get set in place that can change but to effect that change, a lot more repair and alternative experience may be necessary.

The article itself debates the idea that what happens to the infant brain fixes that person's attachment experiences for life. If we believed this were true, we would not be psychotherapists. We are in this field because we care about people and we know the brain is plastic. Experiences throughout life, including the early years, continue to influence a person's development.

Attachment is a biologically-wired aspect of our experience. It is, fundamentally, the way our hypervigilant, environment-scanning reptilian brains are managed by our mammalian brain and our neocortex. It is the way we can feel safe despite the ever-present sense of danger that an infant or young child can experience.

Stephen Porges, in his Polyvagal Theory, discusses attachment as "the path to safety," (Buczynski and Porges, 2012). From this perspective, attachment reflects how a caregiver regulates the early internal experiences of a young child. The path to safety, therefore, will be enhanced or diminished by the quality of early caregiving. A caregiver can help or can miss the mark in regulating an infant's normal dysregulated emotional states of anxiety, terror, and uncertainty. These are "normal" states because the environment to an infant is not understandable. There is no developed neocortex to cognitively make sense of sensate experience such as wetness, hunger, cold, or thirst: There is only sensation that feels good or bad. The neocortex that is available to mediate the environment and know how to provide relief is that of the caregiver. Through their attunement, attention, comfort and soothing, caregivers regulate these dysregulated states of the infant.

As a child grows, neural pathways of chronic regulation or dysregulation are encoded into the infant's brain. Sensitive periods of brain growth and pruning during the first few years and then again in adolescence determine whether the pathways that are developed represent a sense of security or insecurity.

74

Look at the image below. The article, from the *Early Arts* website (http://earlyarts. co.uk/philosophy/creativity-early-brain-development/) states, "This image shows the stark reality of getting it wrong – the CT scan of the brain on the right is that of a three-year-old who has been denied all the natural creative and sensory experiences of the healthy three-year-old child on the left. See how small her brain has shrunk due to the harsh pruning activity that has taken place as a result of those denied opportunities and lack of stimulating experiences…"

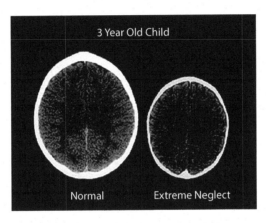

In fact, studies show that the connection between infant and mother starts as early as the third trimester of pregnancy where the fetus reacts to the unique voice of its mother. The infant is born with the brainstem intact (instinct, autonomic somatic activity such as heart rate, respiration, and response to the environment). The limbic system comes on board at birth and is the primary system that is developing over the first two years of life. The development of the cerebral cortex is put on hold until some time in the second year in order to allow the limbic system to develop.

On a cellular level, newborns have 100 billion neurons, the same as an adult but without the same number of synaptic connections. Synaptic connections are established chemically and electrically between neurons. They account for the growth and development of a healthy brain and mind through set neural pathways. Synapses are essentially the gaps between neurons that are used for the chemical and/or electrical transmission of messages within the brain and from the brain to the body. Electrical impulses and chemical neurotransmitters travel in the synapses, connecting receptor cells in each neuron to others.

Each of the 100 billion neurons has 7,000-10,000 possible synaptic connections. For newborns, only one-quarter of the synaptic connections that can be made are already made. The brain, assuming an adequate environment for growth, has much work left to accomplish.*

Over the first two years, growth is rapid. The graphic below gives us a sense of the pace of growth.

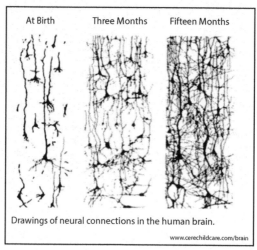

Drawings of neural connections in the human brain.

www.cerechildcare.com/brain

In order to have normal brain growth and normal physical/emotional development, synaptic connections must form. The synaptic connections present at birth allow autonomic activity such as breathing and reflexive attachment behaviors such as reaching to take place.

Since a child cannot survive with breathing alone, wired-in attachment behaviors of caregivers and infants are present to ensure the survival and growth of the infant. The attunement between infant and caregiver fosters the multiplying of synaptic connections the infant will need to grow physically, develop emotionally and learn cognitively. If either the infant or the caregiver fails to demonstrate and utilize these behaviors, psychological

---

* All of the above information is taken from Badenoch, 2011; Hanson, 2009; Siegel, 1999; Cozolino, 2002; and Schore, 2012.

and sometimes physical survival is at stake.

Below, again, are some of the neurobiological attachment behaviors for the infant:

a. Moro reflex (open hands and legs)

b. eyegazing

c. seeking the nipple

d. clinging

e. first and early smiles

f. following with the eyes

g. mimicking mother's facial expressions

h. crying

i. laughing

For the caregiver, instinctive and largely unconscious attachment behaviors include:

j. using sing-song "mothereze"

k. continuous eyegazing

l. awareness of infant at all times

m. reaching for and holding infant against the heart

n. internal distress when the infant is distressed

o. joy when infant responds or laughs

p. physical play with infant

q. responsive facial expressions

These are all limbic system, somatic, automatic attachment behaviors that regulate nervous system activation and go far beyond the provision of food or attending to physical needs.

Although brains are plastic, there are clear "sensitive periods" that are crucial for infant and young child development. The first period is from age 0 – 2. Growth of synaptic connections during the first two years lays the groundwork for continued positive development throughout childhood and into adulthood. Because the right-brain limbic system and implicit memory develop rapidly during this time, the caregiver's ability to attune to the infant in order to facilitate integrated attachment security is essential. Critical neural pathways with encoded messages about self and others are laid down during these years.

Growth of the right-brain limbic system as anticipated leads to the next "sensitive period," starting age two to three: neocortical development of left-brain functions of language, thought, explicit memory, and rational and critical thinking. This period of cortical, linguistic expansion from 24 to 36 months is marked by a child's vocabulary growth from 50 words to 1000 words, complete sentence building and verbal interpersonal communication.

This increase in brain development is accompanied by the disappearance of reflexes. The middle prefrontal cortex fibers expand and extend into the limbic system and brainstem, which enables the child to regulate emotion, receive soothing and self-soothe.

A third "sensitive period" is adolescence where there is a new wave of nerve cell and synaptic connection development. This period mimics the first two years: The limbic system predominates, and the neocortex grows at a slower pace. Development during this period is strongly influenced by a hormonal wash that leaves the adolescent vulnerable to dysregulation and attendant behaviors such as poor reasoning and judgment. Because of this, secure relationships with parents, teachers, therapists or other secure peers is critical at this time.

From the article in *Early Arts*:

> "...Between the age of three and sexual maturity in adolescence, the synapses that are underused start to get pruned out, brain growth slows down, and connections are harder to make in areas that have been pruned, although not impossible. This ensures that the connections that are regularly used get stronger, and those that aren't used are cut back, so the brain effectively becomes more efficient.

> "There are windows of 'plasticity' later on in life where the conditions for learning are positive and connections can be reformed in the brain. However, the prime time to develop specific knowledge, skills and competencies is in the first few years of a child's life.

"...In the early years, neglect and other adverse experiences can have a profound effect on how children are emotionally 'wired'. This will deeply influence their emotional responses to events and their ability to form attachments or to empathize with other people."

Let's take a closer look at the physiology of attachment regulation. Stephen Porges' Polyvagal Theory* articulates the critical role played in attachment by the Vagus Nerve (10th Cranial Nerve) of the parasympathetic nervous system. As we know, the Vagus Nerve has two important branches involved with regulation and dysregulation generally. They are equally important in terms of attachment regulation. Remember that the myelinated branch, called the Ventral Vagus, reflects the Window of Tolerance where there is a sense of safety. And, the nonmyelinated branch is the Dorsal Vagal, which represents hypoarousal reactions of shutdown, shame, dissociation and helplessness.

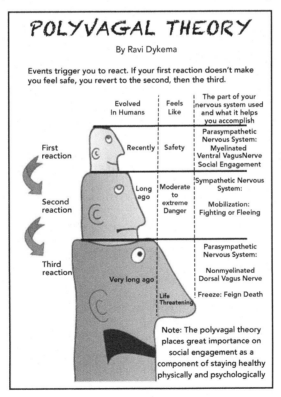

---

* Information about The Polyvagal Theory taken from http://files.nicabm.com/Trauma2012/Porges/NICABM-Porges-2012.pdf, Wikipedia, and Badenoch, 2011.

As the preceding graphic shows, when we feel stress or threat, we first seek safety through attachment and social engagement (Ventral Vagal Complex of the parasympathetic nervous system). When that avenue fails us, we then move into nervous system mobilization responses of fight or flight (Sympathetic Nervous System). However, if the threat is life-threatening and there is no escape or is experienced as such, we then unconsciously depend on the Dorsal Vagal Complex of the parasympathetic nervous system.

According to Bonnie Badenoch in *Being a Brain-Wise Therapist*, the Ventral Vagus "inhibits the fight/flight response of the sympathetic system and allows social engagement/secure attachment to unfold... This myelinated branch runs from brainstem to heart and is involved in perception of facial expressions, the sound of the voice, and the capacity for attuned listening..."

The return to safety is physiologically facilitated through the voice, the ears, the gaze, and facial expression. Nerves controlling muscles in the face and head are mediated by the Ventral Vagus Nerve. According to Porges, "Humans are social beings who have to convey to one another that we're safe to come close to, to hug, and in some cases, have sex with. To convey this message of safety, we utilize the newest vagal circuit to downregulate our sympathetic defenses and present cues of safety when it is appropriate." (NICABM-Porges, 2012)

He explains further that the ventral vagal circuit is expressive and receptive. Muscles of the face and head of the caregiver and the child are responding to information passed from one to the other. These are the muscles involved with the vocal cords, the smile, dilation of the pupils, maintenance of eye contact, and the reception of speech sounds through the middle ears.

What does regulating the ANS mean in this context? For infants, all of whom lack a developed neocortex, the environment is fraught with interpersonal and intrapersonal dangers. Infants have the sensations of hunger, coldness, wetness, loud noises, and sudden movements as well as sensations of a comforting touch, soft voices and warm breath without understanding what it is. There is no knowledge that things that feel bad will be relieved or that things that feel good will be continued. For the infant, the security that they will be taken care of physically and emotionally is totally other-dependent and unconscious.

It is for this reason that infant and caregiver attachment behaviors are hard-wired, reciprocal and contingent. And, it is why the internal sense of security that is laid down or not laid down in neural networks occurs so early in life. The use of the caregiver's well-developed neocortex makes attachment possible.

If a child achieves that internal, unconscious sense that the world is generally safe and they are not alone, neural networks continue to grow and be pruned appropriately which leads to proper growth of the neocortex. This is what we call integration.

An infant with an attuned caregiver will learn the following aspects of emotional intelligence and attachment security:

    a. stress tolerance

    b. tolerance of a broad range of emotions

    c. ability to take risks

    d. trust that the world is essentially safe

    e. ability to love and connect with relative ease

    f. empathy and compassion for self and others

    g. positive sense of self and others

By contrast, when there is inadequate regulation, infants and children will unconsciously encode messages of:

    a. shame and self-disgust

    b. inadequate self-esteem, self-worth

    c. fear of taking risks

    d. chronic sense of intrapersonal and interpersonal danger

    e. not feeling welcomed in the world

    f. anticipation of rejection

    g. inability to engage in a mutual, empathic fashion

    h. helplessness

The Polyvagal Theory underscores attachment as affect regulation and the creation of a clear, unconscious orientation towards the path to safety. As therapists, our job is to help our clients self-regulate and to accept the comfort of co-regulation. In so doing, their brains will begin to develop a conscious orientation to the path to safety. We must also consider how we can self-regulate effectively and efficiently so we become the secure base our clients need.

Right Brain/Left Brain and Attachment

Healthy psychological development depends on adequate intrapersonal and interpersonal affect regulation that then leads to attachment security. Evolution has adapted human brain structures to facilitate this development utilizing a division of labor between the right and left hemispheres.

The right hemisphere, responsible for emotion, implicit memory, and procedural learning, needs to integrate with the left hemisphere which is responsible for language, thought, analysis, and explicit memory. Integration has two aspects: vertical and horizontal. Vertical integration refers to the fiber growth and synaptic connections amongst the three sub-brain structures: brainstem, limbic system, and neocortex. When there is adequate vertical integration, normal electrochemical communication is possible. For humans, this means the brainstem initiates autonomic nervous system responses to threat or danger which then activate appropriate thalamus, hypothalamus and amygdala responses mediated by the hippocampus and neocortex. When there is vertical integration, we are somatically awake to sense threat or danger, we automatically seek a path of safety as the limbic system responds, and we can regulate our fear as we quickly and accurately appraise what is truly dangerous and what is not. All three brains are working together.

Daniel Siegel, in *Pocket Guide to Interpersonal Neurobiology*, writes, "When we become aware of input from the body, the brainstem, and the limbic areas, we combine these subcortical signals with the vertically higher cortical regions to have this form of reflective awareness. Why would anyone not have access to the wisdom of the body, to the regulation and protection of the survival reflexes of the brainstem, and to the evaluative, emotional and attachment-focused limbic processing? One reason is attachment history. If the relationships you may have had were not attuned, the signals from your body may never have been seen by others, and, in fact, you may have felt overwhelmed by the unfulfilled needs emanating from the subcortical regions….Our nonverbal, nonrational, body-based subcortical signals form a crucial foundation for knowing what has meaning in our lives. Impairments to vertical integration often shut down the sense of vitality in life." (Siegel, 2013, p 41-8)

Horizontal (or bilateral) integration involves the communication across the corpus callosum between the right and left brains. Such communication results from fully and normally developed hemispheres and an intact corpus callosum. With horizontal integration, we have a coherent life narrative in a linguistic thought form that incorporates all the somatic, perceptive and emotional information from the right-brain. This coherent narrative corresponds with an earned secure attachment. And, there is a balance between left analytic mode and right stress-regulating and aliveness mode. Again, Daniel Siegel says, "Bilateral integration utilizes both the left and right modes of processing as the two sides of the brain work collaboratively with each other. This form of integration also reveals how one mode may become dominant to the exclusion of the other in the experiences of everyday life." (Siegel, 2013, p. 41-7) In this context, we can more clearly see the internal functioning of an avoidant tendency, dominated by left-brain activity, compared to an anxious/preoccupied tendency, often overwhelmed by the right side.

Vertical Integration	Horizontal Integration
Sensing threat/danger and regulating	Using language to understand self/relationships
Automatically seeking a path to safety	Creating a coherent narrative
Being able to know and feel	Earning a secure attachment

Chapter 10

New Theory of Attachment — Primary and Secondary Systems

Attachment theory has advanced over the last thirty to forty years since Bowlby, Ainsworth and Main researched and confirmed the primacy of attachment in mental health. Their work led to the naming of four styles, an awareness of the prevalence of these styles, and two assessment tools: The Strange Situation and the Adult Attachment Interview.

Research essentially shows the following incidence levels of the four attachment styles with some but not highly significant differences amongst cultures. (The exception would be in countries where war, trauma and forced family separation are constant: This will increase the percentages of all three insecure styles.)

a. Autonomous (Secure): 55% - 65%

b. Dismissing (Avoidant): 20%

   Etiology = harsh, judgmental caregiver; infant/child organizes around dismissing own and others' needs.

c. Preoccupied (Anxious): 10% - 15%

   Etiology = inconsistent caregiving; infant/child insecure about whether needs will or will not be met; emotional needs of parents supercede needs of the infant/child.

d. Unresolved (Disorganized): 5%

Etiology = unresolved grief and trauma of caregiver; abuse; neglect; caregiver untreated rage or depression; infant/child both needs and is terrified by the caregiver.

Use of the concept of styles is still highly prevalent and effective amongst mental health practitioners, educators, and medical professionals. More recent neuroscience, however, has led us to understand the physiological underpinnings of attachment. This understanding incorporates the concept of neuroplasticity of the brain, allowing for later-life brain structure development and integration that affords intrapersonal and interpersonal growth. Allan Schore writes in *The Science of the Art of Psychotherapy*:

Bowlby stated that attachment behavior was based on the need for safety and a secure base. We have demonstrated that attachment is more than this; it is the essential matrix for creating a right-brain self that can regulate its own states and external relationships. Attachment intersubjectivity allows psychic structure to be built and shaped into a unique human being. Our task as therapists is to understand and facilitate this developmental process with our clients. (2012, p. 44)

In this new model, secure attachment is understood as the primary system in correspondence with the ventral vagal circuit. Insecure attachment corresponds with activation of the sympathetic nervous system or the dorsal vagal circuit. Rather than seeing a person as having one attachment style, new views of attachment theory focus on which system is being activated at any given moment. Many of us will spend significant time in the primary system and only move into a secondary system under conditions of perceived interpersonal threat. One goal of therapy is to facilitate a client's ability to spend more time in the primary system and relying less on secondary systems.

Most of us have a tendency toward one secondary system during times of interpersonal (and intrapsychic) stress but there are also times when we might rely on a different secondary system.

A more anxious, preoccupied system is referred to as a hyperactivating system, again following the language of hyperarousal. Here the sympathetic nervous system is activated and produces unconscious strategies of anxiety, clinging, obsessiveness, worry, impulsiveness, rage, and hypervigilance.

A more avoidant, dismissing system is referred to as a deactivating system. This language follows the language of dysregulation we studied earlier: The parasympathetic nervous system, using the Dorsal Vagus, is deactivated and moves the person into unconscious strategies of shut-down, shame, freeze, submit, dissociation, and disconnection.

Disorganized attachment can be a chronic state for very dysregulated clients. Most often, however, the disorganized system is superimposed on another more predominant system that could be secure or insecure. Let's look at the flow chart on the right* for a depiction of the attachment process:

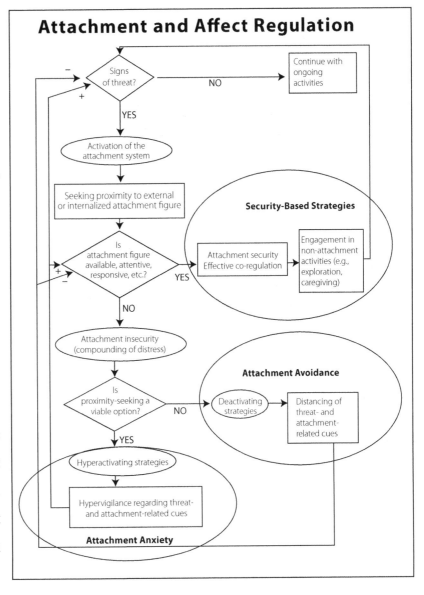

* Attachment theory and affect regulation: The dynamics, development and cognitive consequences of attachment-related strategies; Mikulincer, M., Shaver, P, and Pereg, D., in *Motivation and Emotion*, Vol. 27, #2, June, 2003, page 81.

Note the unconscious decision tree we go through in seeking safety through attachment. As we talked about before in discussing the Polyvagal Theory, there is a descending order of the systems used.

When stressed or threatened, we first assert attachment-seeking behaviors of reaching out to an attachment figure (proximity-seeking). If a safe, effective attachment figure (external or internalized) is available, we feel secure, comforted and relieved, and can return to normal life activities. If a safe, effective attachment figure is not available, we then utilize a hyperactivating system, continuing to seek proximity and comfort unsuccessfully and becoming increasingly distressed. Finally, an ongoing lack of a safe, effective attachment figure is experienced as life-threatening and we then utilize a deactivating system.

Notice that the hyperactivating system still holds the possibility of relief if a reliable attachment figure can be located. However, a hyperactivating system can get physiologically locked into a cycle of continuous activation, as noted on the bottom of the chart: continued "hypervigilance regarding threat-and attachment-related cues."

In contrast with the hyperactivating system, the deactivating system results in a quicker sense of giving up and leaving the person still experiencing signs of threat. The diagram shows a chronic giving up on the possibility of connection, safety and needs being met: continued "distancing of threat-and-attachment-related cues."

If our work with an avoidant-tending client leads to more attachment anxiety, we would consider that progress towards the ultimate goal of relative security. The following example illustrates this.

CASE EXAMPLE

During the first session with a client, he had difficulty making eye contact and expressed nausea in being in therapy and with the feeling that he had to be there. Presenting problems were chronic depression and difficulties with intimacy with his wife. Over time, he also expressed how hard it was to be in the room and that he felt spaced out at times while with me. He came late and occasionally called at the last minute to cancel.

I spent a lot of time letting him know he was in control of sessions, what we talked about, and for how long. He talked about interpersonal problems in his life but, if we touched a vulnerable area, he would dissociate. I would then suggest we talk about current events and movies, which we would do for chunks of time. My only therapeutic interventions at this point were having us acknowledge we were doing that and asking how it affected him in his body. When he came back into his body enough, he was able to notice that the nausea had receded and he did not feel as vulnerable. Later, after he was more regulated, I explained the Window of Tolerance so he could understand what was happening in his nervous system.

Over time, his relationship to me started to shift. He talked about not wanting to come in to therapy because he thought he was disappointing me, that there was something fundamentally flawed about him, and that he wasn't making enough progress for me. He wondered if he was a good enough client for me.

This shift in his acknowledgment of concern about how I felt about him came to a head when I had to be out for six weeks due to a family emergency. Although I said I would contact him as soon as I could come back and gave him a range of time, he contacted me first because he was in crisis. As we worked with the crisis, he talked about his anxiety that I hadn't called him because I really didn't want to work with him, and he disclosed for the first time that he felt dependent on the therapy.

Along with reassurance, I also used psychoeducation and talked about attach-

ment, suggesting that concern for how I felt about him actually represented a movement towards more security: He was letting himself be aware he had needs for connection and beginning to express them and act on them.

Awareness of which strategy or system clients use on a moment-to-moment basis, coupled with awareness of our own strategies, will enhance and deepen the therapy.

Post-Test: Neuroscience of Attachment

1. Is secure attachment a primary or secondary system? Why?

   _____

   _____

2. True or False: A person's attachment style may change somewhat during the course of life but it is essentially fixed as a result of early caregiving experiences.

3. What are the two periods of intense limbic development for humans where the limbic system and nonverbal, right-brain experiences predominate over the neocortex and left-brain experiences?

   _____   _____

4. How does secure attachment protect us?

   _____

   _____

5. Right-brain and bilateral integration is critical for children to learn how to deal with threat and danger. Match the following brain functions with the processes and structures they depend on by choosing from the following terms: brain stem; limbic system; neocortex;

Brain structures:

   a. Sensing threat or danger _____

   b. Using language to explain what happened to you

   _____

   c. Automatically seeking a path to safety_____

   d. Being able to know and feel things are okay even if you get scared

   _____

   e. Creating a coherent narrative _____

   f. Earning a secure attachment _____

Match the integration processes below by choosing from the following terms: right-brain vertical integration; right-left brain horizontal integration.

Integration processes:

   a. Sensing threat or danger _____

   b. Using language to explain what happened to you

   _____

   c. Automatically seeking a path to safety _____

   d. Being able to know and feel things are okay even if you get scared

   _____

  e. Creating a coherent narrative _____

  f. Earning a secure attachment _____

6. There is a specific nerve that is involved in attachment and is a part of the Autonomic Nervous System. What is this nerve called?

  _____

7. Myelin is a fibrous covering of cerebrospinal nerves that facilitates fast and accurate transmission of nerve messages to different parts of the brain. What is the myelinated part of the specific nerve called?

  _____. What is the nonmyelinated part of the specific nerve called?_____

8. Name some instinctual attachment behaviors that the mother or primary caregiver demonstrates:_____

9. If the child has good-enough parenting such that secure attachment is achieved in the first two years, what important integrated skills has the child learned? _____

  _____

10. What is the difference between the kind of learning that happens in the first two years and the kind of learning that happens when neocortical development accelerates? _____

  _____

  Name which hemisphere of the brain is mostly responsible for each kind of learning. 1. _____ 2. _____

11. True or False: Limbic system development is primarily unconscious, non-verbal and visceral.

Part III
Somatic Attachment Therapy and Skills

Chapter 11

Stance of the Therapist

Somatic Attachment Therapy aims to provide a transformative experience for clients based on body-brain integration through the use of present moment attachment tracking. In this regard, attending to the body is equally as important as attending to thoughts or emotions. And, attending to what is happening with our own attachment activation is equally as important as attending to our clients' activation. Likewise, attending to what makes us and our clients feel alive is equally as important as what causes pain and suffering. We sit with our clients as human beings and as guides. We use our whole selves in our relationships with them as they seek to heal and become their authentic selves.

The following page is a chart outlining key aspects of Somatic Attachment Therapy so readers can note differences with other approaches.

Following the chart are the organizing principles of Somatic Attachment Therapy, basic somatic skills, chapters on our attachment strategies, and how to work with attachment in therapy.

Category	Somatic Attachment Therapy
Goal of Therapy:	Earned secure attachment; coherent life narrative
Attitude to client:	Equality; compassion; loving-kindness
Methods/Focus:	Curiosity; self-study; somatic tracking; attachment bubble; accepting not knowing; tracking own responses
View of Defenses:	Support; see as wise protections; explore
View of Boundaries:	Less tight; looser in service of authenticity/connection
Self-disclosure:	Some to high as part of organic process
Therapist sees self as:	Helpful/knowledgeable companion on journey; secure attachment figure
View of character/personality:	Protective organizing strategies
View of causality:	Organization of early and ongoing experience; attachment insecurity
Dysregulation Focus:	Some to very high
What happens in session:	Moment by moment body tracking; child state; affect regulation; building secure attachment
Fields of experience:	Body; core beliefs; emotion; resources; relationship
Resourcing:	High focus
Stance of therapist:	Open; ok with not knowing; exploring as process unfolds
Use of Touch	Used with caution, permission and constant tracking

Chapter 12

MENCAP:
Principles of Somatic Attachment Therapy

—————

M: Mindfulness as observation

Mindfulness has different meanings in different contexts. Somatic Attachment Therapy has a specific meaning and method: observation of internal experience alone or in relationship for the purpose of self-study and regulation.

E: Embodied Awareness

Somatic Attachment Therapy begins with the concept that our bodies have information to give us we cannot access through our thoughts alone. Body information reflects unconscious, habitual patterns of emotional and relational organization neurologically stored when our cognitive brain structures were not developed or not adequately matured. Exploring the body enables us to observe these patterns in action to make them conscious and available for change.

N: Neuroplastician

We, as therapists, are braingrowers. The compassionate and secure relationship with the therapist literally facilitates the growing and strengthening of fibers and synaptic connections between the right brain and the left brain and between the three different brain structures of each hemisphere. Therapeutic interventions either reinforce or enable the freeing of stuck relational and intrapersonal patterns of emotional organization. The most effective therapists recognize they are neuroplasticians and can visualize and kinesthetically experience clients' brains changing as they work together.

C: Compassion

Compassion for self and for the client is the most essential ingredient of any therapy. Compassion assumes any client behavior has an historic, emotional, and often unconscious root and reason. Therefore, what may be thought of as maladaptive behaviors are first and foremost seen as necessary, unconscious protections. Use of the word "resistance" contradicts compassion and a basic neuro-emotional understanding of human behavior. Compassion assumes goodwill, respect, and essential loving-kindness towards the client and towards self.

A: Attachment Bubble

The goal of this psychotherapy is to help the client earn a secure attachment and to develop a coherent narrative of their life experience. The attachment bubble helps the therapist recognize which attachment strategy has been activated for them and for the client at any given moment. Imaging the bubble and feeling the sense of being inside or outside of the bubble facilitates the therapist's moment-to-moment connectedness with the client. Using the attachment bubble necessitates therapist somatic self-awareness, self-regulation, and recognition of their own attachment strategies.

P: Permission-seeking

Somatic Attachment Therapy assumes the client knows more about their experience than we as therapists do. The primary change vehicle is the client awakening to their own experience without imposition. Seeking permission from clients regarding the use of any techniques or interpretations is vital to the building of trust and to developing the client's sense of agency. Labeling and diagnostic impressions have limited use and can impede building a secure attachment.

Chapter 13

The Neuroscience and Theory of Tracking

With this chapter, we move into somatic skills necessary to work with body-mind integration. Much of the skills taught in this section are derived from the concepts and teachings of Ron Kurtz and his Hakomi Body-Centered Psychotherapy. Some of these skills are also used in other somatic-focused trainings and some are an integration of all of my learning, training, and experience with clients.

We start with tracking. Tracking is the most basic skill and one that is used by therapists across all disciplines. The difference lies in what is tracked.

CBT therapists track responses to interventions. Psychodynamic therapists track emotions, transference, and process. Narrative therapists track beliefs that underlie stories. Each discipline uses its theory and approach to determine what needs to be noticed and enhanced.

In Somatic Attachment Therapy, as well as all body-oriented psychotherapies, tracking is extremely broad and includes somatic, emotional, cognitive, energetic, and intrapersonal and interpersonal fields.

We are concerned with tracking the client verbally and nonverbally, focusing more on the person in the moment rather than on the story. In particular, we are focused on the live experience of the client as it unfolds in the room with us on a moment-to-moment basis.

When we track all of the dimensions while the client is talking, both client and therapist have access to information that has not previously been available. This information is stored in unconscious early right-brained neural networks called hidden layers. (Cozolino, 2002)

Hidden layers are the networks that were laid down in our brains during the first one and one-half to two years of our lives and then reinforced throughout our lifetimes. Genetics, psychosocial impacts and later life events are factors also but this first early period is universally critical.

Life experiences during the first two years are visceral and nonverbal; we can't access them through our cognition and verbal language alone. Somatic Attachment Therapy tracks for those hidden layers of synaptic connections and neural pathways that have been laid down and organized during those early years, then reinforced.

For example, if an infant/child is treated with empathy, comfort, and support, the synaptic connections between neurons that link Window of Tolerance physiology with interactions with another person are enhanced. Window of Tolerance physiology includes calm breathing and heart rate, even body temperature, and the ability to perceive with all senses and to respond reasonably to stress.

If a child is belittled, the neural pathways of safety and connection are not used and are pruned, replaced by fragments of connections not completed or entire pathways of shame and fear. This physiology reflects not feeling safe or at ease: fast or slow heart rate, hyperalert or hypoalert to danger, tense muscles, and body temperature changes.

Furthermore, early attachment behaviors designed as a survival mechanism to protect the infant are activated or deactivated during this period. Therefore, core beliefs such as "I am safe, loved, and free to be myself," or "I am alone and no one can help me" are formed. Our work is to track those beliefs as they manifest through the client's conscious and unconscious expression and presentation.

What Exactly Do We Track?

1. Facial expressions: movements on any part of the face; discrepancy between words and expression; tense vs. relaxed; eyes wide or narrowed; nose flared; color changes; lips pursed, twisted.

2. Eye contact: direct, averted, changing: looking down; eyes flitting; gaze right or left; sustained or strained gaze.

3. Breathing: held, shallow or deep; sighing; changes in breathing pattern.

4. Hand gestures: repeated gesture; part of the body being touched or held.

5. Movements of any part of body: micromovements; finger tapping; foot tapping; stroking hair.

6. Location of body in space: forward or back in chair; posture slumped or upright, rigid or easy.

7. Quality of energy: agitated, flowing, cut off; muscle tone; heavy or light.

8. Speech quality: tone of voice, inflection; soft, loud; measured, staccato, halting; changeable; two-person interaction or one person interaction.

9. Quality of narrative: tangential; concentrating; clear or confusing.

10. Mental states: in or out of body; labile or stable; sense of presence, lack of presence (dissociation).

TRACKING EXERCISE: (Client not in Mindfulness)

1. A client sits in front of you, smiling and nodding her head slightly. Her left foot is kicking almost imperceptibly. She sits forward in her chair, and says quickly, "Most of my therapy experiences have not been so good. But I heard great things about you so…" Her voice drifts off so you barely hear her. She looks up at you, then away, then back.

As you read this, write what you track in terms of the following:
   a. Voice quality _____
   b. Energy _____
   c. Congruence_____
   d. Eye Contact _____
   e. Movement _____

As you imagine the above, consider what else you might track for as the session continues: _____

2. You are working with a heterosexual couple in their fifties. They have seen you a number of times for issues of emotional and sexual intimacy. As the man talks, you notice the woman is sitting tightly and her eyes are fixed on him. His face is flushed, his voice slightly raised, and he looks at a space right above her face. His body is turned away from hers somewhat. "You are so worried about the kids all the time. What about me?" As he speaks, she takes in a breath and seems to hold it while he continues, his voice rising. "I work so hard, have given you everything, yet I seem to come last."

As you read this, write what you track in terms of the following:

    a. Physical reactions to each other _____

    b. Breathing patterns _____

    c. Regulation/dysregulation_____

    d. Voice quality _____

    e. Eye Contact _____

As you imagine the above, consider what else you might track for as the session continues: _____

TRACKING EXERCISE: (Client in Mindfulness)

Client 1:

A client breathes out several times, then sighs. His hands, previously clasped, seemed to have loosened some. He says, softly, "My chest feels lighter."

What do you track in the following areas:

    a. Shifts_____

    b. Voice quality_____

    c. Body states/movements _____

The client's eyes are squeezed tight. Tears are forming in his eyes. He reaches for a Kleenex, wipes them away. "No need to cry," he says, opening his eyes.

What do you track in the following areas:

    a. Facial expression/movements_____

    b. Congruence_____

    c. State of consciousness _____

    —

Client 2:

Her eyes are closed. Her mouth is set tightly and her jaw seems tense. She says in an agitated voice, "I notice a lot of thoughts, an image is coming up of my mother in her pajamas, she's pacing, maybe I'm four, I don't know, maybe we're in Fresno, oh, no, must be in Bakersfield by then, then we moved to Los Angeles, but that was later, the pajamas she's wearing are blue polka dot, I think, and her face is close to mine, she's saying something in a loud voice…"

What do you track in the following areas:

     a. Voice quality: _____

     b. Quality of Narrative: _____

     c. Quality of Speech: _____

     d. Regulation/Dysregulation: _____

The client stops talking and becomes very quiet. Her body is still, her hands are held tightly against her sides, and her breathing is shallow. Her head starts to look toward the right and drops.

What do you track in the following areas:

     a. Regulation/Dysregulation_____

     b. Body state/position_____

     c. Energy _____

     d. Shifts_____

Chapter 14

Tracking and Contacting*

Contacting is an essential somatic skill that goes hand in hand with tracking. Contacting entails choosing a specific aspect of the client's experience you are noticing or perceiving and calling their attention to it in a specific way. In order to contact effectively, it is necessary to track accurately and non-interpretively.

Contacting begins with a verbal or nonverbal reflecting back to the client what you track. Often, you name something the client is not aware of. For example, he is holding his breath. "You seem to be holding your breath."

As you name something not necessarily known by the client, the client feels seen (see sections on Attachment later which explore the various ways this can be received.) As your contact statement brings this into the client's awareness, you then track what happens next. Sometimes, there is recognition, "Oh, yeah, I guess I am." Or it might not be right. Since tracking is continuously happening, the therapist then has an opportunity to contact the reaction. Suppose the client says, "No, I don't think so…" with voice trailing off. A contact statement might be, "That wasn't exactly right, huh?"

Contact statements often start outside of mindfulness and are amplified very precisely during mindfulness. Here is an example including deepening, a skill we will learn next.

---

* Hakomi terms and skills

Therapist: "I notice your hands moving quickly as you say that."

Contact statement

Client: "Oh, I wasn't aware of that."

Therapist: "Would it be okay to explore what they might be saying?"

Getting permission

Client: "Okay" (nodding)

Therapist helps client become mindful.

Inducing and managing consciousness

Therapist: "So, let's have you move your hands just as you were doing, and notice what happens."

Deepening

Client moves hands quickly and, spontaneously, starts to slow down.

Therapist: "Oh, slowing down now."

Contact statement

Client: "Yeah, I'm feeling a little sad."

Therapist: "Yeah, is it ok to stay with that sad feeling?"

Deepening with permission-seeking

To be effective, a contact statement is short, descriptive, non-interpretive, and seeks corroboration from the client. If, in the example above, the therapist says, "You seem anxious, your hands are moving so quickly," the client might then respond, "Well, I had some coffee before I came here" or, "I don't know, maybe I'm anxious." Or, "Yes, I'm anxious. I am always anxious."

This therapist statement, "You seem anxious, your hands are moving so quickly," can be used effectively in many therapies. In the context of somatic work, however, the interpretive statements move the client out of their own internal and physical experience to then cognitively evaluate the accuracy of your statement. In the interpretive example above, the therapist has called attention to something being expressed and moved it in a particular way. In so doing, the therapist could be blocking exploration of the physical, more implicit, more limbic experience.

When we work in mindfulness, we are looking to help the client explore with curiosity and non-judgment their organic process and see where it leads on its own. In the dialogue on the preceding page, here the therapist's tracking and contacting led to a particular client movement; the movement could have meant excitement, anxiety, worry, traumatic activation, etc. Contacting without interpretation lets the process unfold.

As noted above, you don't need to worry about making mistakes. If you say something and it doesn't fit for the client, you just recalibrate, "Oh, not quite right," then track and contact again.

This skill of nondefensively allowing for being "wrong" and acknowledging it to the client not only helps the two of you get back on track but, more importantly, it conveys a desire for attunement and a willingness to repair, a cornerstone of attachment.

How to Make a Contact Statement:

There are four structural aspects to contacting:

a. *Choosing what to contact:* Choose the most salient, alive, "juicy" thing you notice. What jumps out at you? What is your gut noticing?

b. *Crafting the right contact statement:* Find a concise, direct, and to-the-point way of making the statement. Rather than, "It seems to me you might be feeling kind of awkward because you are fidgeting", say instead, "I notice some fidgeting," or "Your hands have a lot of energy, huh?"

c. *Delivering:* Find an appropriate time and an appropriate tone of voice to deliver the contact statement. Assess where the client is…are they ready to be contacted? Or, for example, is the client deep in mindfulness, processing something and needing some space? Is the client waiting for something from you? Does there seem to be something the client is not aware of?

Use a tone of voice that conveys curiosity, non-judgment, warmth, allows for correction, and offers a sense of "We are in this together."

d. *Re-tracking:* Any contact statement needs to be immediately followed by close tracking. Notice what happens after you offer the statement. Does the client move into more thinking? Does the client nod and say, "Yeah, you're right. I wasn't noticing that."? Does the client shake their head and then open their eyes?

All of the above is in service of greater empathic attunement, assessing for dysregulation, developing attachment, and promoting self-study on the part of the client.

TRACKING AND CONTACTING EXERCISE:

Let's look at the tracking vignettes again and determine what might be appropriate contact statements:

Client 1:

A client breathes out several times, then sighs. His hands, previously clasped, seemed to have loosened some. He says, softly, "My chest feels lighter."

Choose a good contact statement (pick all that would work):

a. "Lighter, huh?"

b. "Something's shifted."

c. "You're feeling less anxious, huh?"

d. "Why do you think your chest was tight?"

e. "What are you feeling right now?"

f. "Your whole body looks different."

The client's eyes are squeezed tight. Tears are forming in his eyes, he reaches for a

Kleenex, wipes them away. "No need to cry," he says, opening his eyes.

Choose a good contact statement (pick all that would work):

a. "It's okay to cry."

b. "Something happened just then."

c. "You're upset."

d. "A lot's happening right now."

e. "Torn, huh? Crying yet not wanting to."

Client 2:

Her eyes are closed. Her mouth is set tightly and her jaw seems tense. She says in an agitated voice, "I notice a lot of thoughts, an image is coming up of my mother in her pajamas, she's pacing, maybe I'm four, I don't know, maybe we're in Fresno, oh, no, must be in Bakersfield by then, then we moved to Los Angeles, but that was later, the pajamas she's wearing are blue polka dot, I think, and her face is close to mine, she's saying something in a loud voice…"

Choose a good contact statement (pick all that would work):

a. "You moved around a lot, huh?"

b. "A lot of memory flashing through you right now."

c. "Your voice is rushed."

d. "What emotion comes up as you see her?"

e. "Her voice is loud."

She stops talking and becomes very quiet. Her body is still, her hands are held tightly against her sides, and her breathing is shallow.. Her head starts to look toward the right and drops.

Choose a good contact statement (pick all that would work):

a. "Just let yourself breathe."

b. "Your breath is shallow."

c. "This is hard, huh?"

d. "You looked to your right."

e. "Something intense is happening right now."

Chapter 15

Slowing[*]

One of the beautiful aspects of working somatically is observing things slowly. When we are talking outside of mindfulness, there are multiple layers of experience happening and flying under the radar of our consciousness. Somatic work enables us to access those layers of experience and make them conscious. When something is conscious, we have an opportunity for understanding, choice, and change.

Keep slowing in mind as you work even if you are not working in mindfulness. Often clients come in and start talking rapidly. It can be useful to just say, "There's a lot happening and this is very important. Is it okay to slow this down a little so I am sure to understand you?"

As you move into using mindfulness, slowing is a critical skill to learn. You can train yourself to key into a client's pace by observing the signs of speed:

    a. A lot of talking/storytelling

    b. Jumping from experience to experience

    c. Seemingly contradictory messages

    d. There doesn't seem to be room for you

---

[*] The concept of slowing down is used broadly in Hakomi. I have identified it here as a separate skill.

Clients speed up for many reasons:

    a. Vulnerability

    b. Information is coming rapidly

    c. Unclear what to do

    d. Fear of being seen or going deeply

    e. Dysregulation

When you help a client slow down in mindfulness, the two of you together can get a clearer sense of what is happening. If the client feels vulnerable, then that feeling (essentially the unseen, unconscious metaprocess) becomes the focus. What does the client need? Do you need to help the client regulate? Do you need to do something to help the client feel less vulnerable? Does the client just need more guidance on how to slow down? Is the client afraid of slowing down?

For most therapists, observing what's happening in yourself will be the most significant way you become aware things are moving too fast in mindfulness. Begin to notice your internal experience as a guide.

- What's happening inside of you? Are you confused or overwhelmed? Have you started thinking rapidly? Do you have racing thoughts? Are you beginning to think, "I don't know what to do."? Are you worrying you are not a good enough therapist in that moment?

- What is happening in your body? Are you getting hyperaroused (worry, obsessive thinking) or hypoaroused (spaced out, feel disconnected, wanting to leave)?

- Checking in with yourself and translating that into a slowing intervention will bring you back into the present. In order to work effectively and safely with clients, you must be in mindfulness and regulated yourself.

SLOWING EXERCISE:

Take a few moments and reflect on a client who tends to speak or move quickly, or a client where you have difficulty tracking because there is tangential speech or quick changes in content, mood, etc. Write here what you notice happening in yourself that indicates you need to help the client slow down.

_____

_____

_____

Write below one or two contact statements you could make to help someone slow down.

_____

_____

_____

Chapter 16

Supporting the Wisdom of Defenses

A s you start working somatically, accepting and honoring client defenses becomes a vital part of the process, another concept pioneered by Ron Kurtz and the Hakomi Method. One aspect of compassionate therapy includes the understanding of the place of defenses in psychological development.

We all organize ourselves unconsciously to maintain physical and psychological safety. By the time we are around two, most of our core beliefs are formed and are then reinforced by our environment. Behaviors that stem from these beliefs are in our bodies' and brains' implicit memory and most often reflect unconscious survival resources. As somatic attachment therapists, we are continuing to look for the manifestations of those beliefs in whatever form they appear.

Let's look at the following example:

A young man looks up at his therapist, smiles quizzically, then turns his head to the right. A traditional process-oriented psychotherapist might say, "I notice you're not looking at me. What makes it hard to look at me?" Even said gently, this intervention confronts the defense in the interest of changing it. Some clients might be able to respond searching for some insight but others may feel increasingly self-conscious or ashamed.

A somatic attachment therapist, in contrast, recognizes the head turn as a survival resource that offers protection. Here, the therapist's goal is to support the defense to reduce shame and to provide a safe manner for exploring it. Noticing the head turn, the therapist might say, "You turned your head. Feels better that way, huh? Just notice what happens in your body when you look away." In this example, we don't know what the head turn means. Further somatic exploration might yield a formerly-unrecognized belief such as, "It's not safe to be seen." Or, it might just enhance his sense of safety so that he can begin to look at his process without having to give up his resource.

Here's a dialogue illustrating supporting the defense.

Client: (in mindfulness) I can feel tears starting to come and I don't want to cry. (Anxious voice, eyes cast downward)

Therapist: That's clear for you. So, just let those tears move back into your eyes to keep them from coming.   Supporting the defense,

Deepening one (See Chapter 16)

Client: (Nodding, voice starting to calm)

Therapist: Your voice is calmer. Yes, let the tears move back, feel them drying as you do that and notice what else is happening in your body.

Deepening one

Client: I'm feeling better, less like I want to cry, but I don't want to focus on my body right now.

Therapist: Ok, let's honor that. What do you think of the woman in the painting here?

Supporting the defense through distraction

Client: I've been looking at that painting, actually, and have been struck by the lightness, the feeling of flying.

Therapist: (Looking at the painting) I see what you mean. And the man, he's got a very flexible neck, doesn't he?   Engaging with client in safe way

by bringing her into present moment

(Both laughing)

Client: (Moving her neck to match the painting) That's hard to do.

Therapist: (Doing the same thing) Impossible. Very whimsical, isn't it?

(Both laughing)

Client: (Sighing, making direct eye contact with the therapist) I feel better now.

Therapist: How do you notice that? What tells you that?

Deepening one

Client: I feel more calm, my voice isn't shaking. I actually notice some tears now but am ok with them.

Therapist: Something shifted.

Contact statement

Client: Your kindness, your helping me not cry, touched me.

Therapist: I can see that. I'm glad it touched you.

Contact statement, attachment joining

Client: I just had a thought: Your supporting me made me feel it's okay to protect myself. (A little surprised, "aha" moment)

Therapist: "It's okay to protect myself." This is important. It is okay to say it again and notice what happens in your body?

Contact statement,
Deepening one

Client: (nodding) "It's okay to protect myself." It feels good, there's a warmth in my chest and a relaxation in my jaw.

Therapist: Let yourself feel that warmth as it spreads through your chest, the jaw relaxing...

Deepening one

Client: Yeah. Wasn't that funny I didn't want to cry before but now the tears are okay? (smiling, looking at therapist)

Therapist: Yeah. (smiling)

Client: Another thought: "To be vulnerable I need to feel safe." Wow, I just had a memory when I said that...."

And the session moves on from there where the client accesses a somatic and emotional imprint of being shamed for being vulnerable. A core belief is now consciously available and able to be worked on.

How do Defenses Show up in Somatic Attachment Work?

Verbally:

Client says: "I don't want to feel this."

Client says: "I feel self-conscious"

Client says: "There's a 'no' coming up when you say that."

Client says: "I can't go there."

Client says: "What is it you want me to do?"

Client says: "I'm afraid to slow things down."

Somatically:

Head turns away

Eye contact is diverted, intermittent

Arms crossed on the chest

Hands make pushing away gesture

Energetically:

Pops out of mindfulness often

Talks a lot from their head

Does not want to try different suggestions made by therapist

How Do We Work with Defenses?

At whatever stage of therapy you are in, defenses can manifest themselves. Respond to the client exactly where they are.

1. Clients who show energetic defenses are usually unable, initially, to stay with mindfulness. Many of these clients will have an avoidant attachment tendency: Slowing things down and looking at internal experience together can make them feel too exposed. To respect this, therapists need to be willing to:

    a. Move slowly.

    b. Do a lot of psychoeducation regarding the wisdom of not exposing themselves and what that might reflect in their nervous system and histories.

    c. Allow for gradual willingness to try small suggestions as they become ready, being mindful to offer permission to stop at any point the client wishes.

    d. Name the positive aspect of the defense as it really is – protection- whenever possible.

    e. Be conscious of your own countertransference of impatience or disconnection.

The client will likely respond better to little bits of mindfulness work as they surface naturally in the session rather than an intentional induction into mindfulness. For example, if the client moves from sitting on the edge of their seat to moving back, you can ask the client to notice how that shift felt.

2. Clients who show verbal and somatic defenses will likely be able to track all of this with you in mindfulness.

    a. Identify quickly to yourself the "defense" and blend it in with your understanding of the naturally-occurring narrative of the client, i.e., "This response is necessary for the client and I am going to support it."

    b. Over time, you will think of these responses less as defenses and will view them more as part of the unfolding of the client's unconscious and transforming process.

c. Verbally contact the client's behavior, movements and words without judgment. Continue to explore the client's own sense of what feels okay to explore or not explore.

d. In the example above, the client didn't want to cry: The therapist not only acknowledges it but actively helps the client not cry.

e. Support of defensive responses most often leads to the client not having to hold on to that defense as the therapist is holding it for the client.

SUPPORTING THE WISDOM OF DEFENSES EXERCISE:

Which of the following therapist responses reflect supporting the defense:

1. *Client:* "I don't want to dig up the past."

    a. "Yes, the past is painful but it is important for us to understand it."

    b. "What are you afraid of?"

    c. "There's a wise part inside you that knows that."

    d. "Let's take this pillow and make it your past. Tell me what I should do with it."

2. You noticed the client was tapping her fingers on her knees and say, "I see you tapping your fingers there." The client turns red, stops tapping her fingers and says, "Just a habit."

    a. "I wonder if you are anxious being here."

    b. "That didn't feel great when I said that, did it? Thanks for letting me know."

    c. Nod and say, "Okay, I'm sorry I interrupted you."

    d. "This is a habit and I appreciate your saying that. The reason I said that is I am looking for what your body might be saying. If you feel comfortable at some point, maybe we can do that together."

3.   A client is working in mindfulness and says, "A wall suddenly came up."

   a.   "Do you think we could take down that wall?"

   b.   "Is there something you don't want to see?"

   c.   "A wall, that's important. Is it okay to stay with that wall?"

   d.   "If the wall had words, what might they be?"

Chapter 17

Deepening One & Deepening Two

———————

As we work with clients in mindfulness, slowly enough to observe and with respect for defenses that may emerge, we begin to offer clients a deeper present-moment experience of how their inner lives have been unconsciously constructed. Deepening is a skill that facilitates the revealing of the complete experience of the client so that all facets can be accessed. It is critical to let the client's organic process unfold. In this manner, we begin to have access to the life experiences that created original unconscious choices, behaviors and patterns of relating. Hakomi uses this same concept through a variety of skills including experiments, probes, immersion, and takeovers. I have revamped them conceptually into two levels of deepening.

Once a sensation, gesture, image, energy, feeling, urge, or memory has been tracked and contacted, the therapist helps the client move further into that particular state by gently guiding the person to experience it more fully.

Deepening One

- Track and contact the client's present moment experience in mindfulness: a gesture, a sigh, a flushed face, repetitive movement -- anything that seems to reflect the unconscious expression of the client's words.

- For example, you notice a client moving her fist in the air (tracking), and you say, "You're moving your fist in the air" (contacting). Wait for some acknowledgement of this. (Sometimes clients will be surprised.) Then deepen that somatic expression: "Would it be okay to just keep doing that gesture and notice what happens?" (deepening and permission-seeking)

- With client agreement, encourage them to just do the gesture and pay attention with curiosity rather than judgment or interpretation.

- As the client starts repeating the gesture, you begin to track and contact again: "A lot of energy there. Is it okay to keep doing that and notice what happens?"

- Continue tracking and contacting the changes that occur until something else emerges.

Deepening One Therapist Suggestions

1. "Stay with that and notice what happens."

2. "Maybe try slowing that down or speeding it up."

3. "Describe the image completely – Where are you? What color is the bedspread? Who's there with you?"

4. "If the gesture had words, what would they be?"

5. "Try saying that again and notice what happens in your body."

6. "Describe the heat in your chest – Is it red-hot? Warm? Spreading?

DEEPENING ONE EXERCISE:

Write a deepening one suggestion for each contact statement below:

1. "Your voice is rushed."

_____

2. "I noticed your hand was moving in circles."

_____

3. "Ah, you're seeing yourself in your room."

_____

4. "Your thumb is moving slowly against your right hand."

_____

5. "Tension in your head, huh?"

_____

6. "There's a lot happening right now."

_____

Deepening Two

Deepening Two involves intensifying the experience through a slight leap into more directiveness. This leap is somewhat intuitive and follows close tracking and sensing. With a little bit of practice, you can learn to sense when something else wants to happen. That is when you use deepening two interventions.

Deepening Two Therapist Suggestions

1. "There's something familiar about this, huh?"

2. "If we give a voice to each part here, what would each part say? I am going to say those sentences to you in a dialogue; just notice what happens."

3. "Let's use these three pillows to represent the three options you just named."

4. "I am going to say a statement to you. Just notice what comes up when I say, 'It is okay to rest.'" (Here, we use the person's name first because it adds intensity. This kind of intervention taps into a person's negative core belief. We say the opposite and see what emerges.)

   Note: This statement is designed to evoke more material for the purpose of exploration. It is not designed to offer reassurance.

5. "Your hand has been holding your chest for a while. What if I came and put my hand on yours to support you?"*

6. "You are holding your head with your hands. What if I held your head for you?"*

---

* As with anything somatic, seeking and getting permission is critical. Whenever a therapist uses touch, getting permission is mandatory. Please read the next chapter, "Special Consideration: Use of Touch."

Chapter 18

Special Consideration: Use of Touch

Working somatically can, but does not have to, involve the use of touch. This chapter intends to address both the implications of using or not using touch with clients.

We are all trained appropriately to keep important boundaries with our clients for their safety. For most therapists, not touching clients falls into this category.

Each therapist needs to think carefully and make a personal decision regarding the use of touch according to comfort level and training. Somatic work allows for the use of touch in a limited, goal-directed, and clearly-delineated manner.

If you decide you are willing to use touch appropriately to deepen the work, here are some guidelines to follow:

a. Know the trauma history of your client so you can determine if touch would be activating.

b. MAKE SURE YOU ARE IN A SECURE, REGULATED STATE YOURSELF BEFORE YOU USE ANY TOUCH.

c. Recognize that touch is an extremely powerful interpersonal connection that can bring up unconscious reactions you can't always predict.

d. Use touch with a clear idea (even if it is based on instinct) where you think it will lead in the particular instance.

e.   Use of touch NEVER means any kind of sexual touch.

f.   CLEAR PERMISSION from the client is essential. You should not proceed unless you have clear permission, which means tracking the client's verbal and nonverbal response to your suggestion. If a client says yes with a wavering voice, say, "Your voice is wavering, are you sure?" If your instinct tells you the client is not sure, do not use touch. It is critical to always track client nonverbal responses regardless of what the client says.

g.   Delineate exactly what kind of touch you will do. "I will put my hand over your hand, is that okay?"

h.   Remember that most clients have their eyes closed at this point. Tell the client exactly what you are doing: "Okay, I am walking over to you now and I am about to put my hand on yours. Is this okay? If anything at all doesn't feel right about this, tell me and I will take my hand away. The most important thing here is your feeling safe."

i.   Check in with client immediately, "Okay, my hand is on yours. Is this okay?" Wait for assent. If none, remove your hand and track/contact what is happening.

j.   If client says it is okay: "What are you noticing?"

k.   Track with your right brain (intuition) if this is truly okay. If you sense the client pull back, wince, or get suddenly extremely quiet, tell the client you are not sure the client feels safe, so you are going to take your hand away.

l.   Follow through with the use of touch in mindfulness to its organic completion using tracking, contacting and deepening one. Usually there is some significant shift that can lead to a transformation in belief: "I don't have to do this alone," or "It's okay to relax."

m.   Withdraw from touch with the permission of the client when the completion has happened. Be mindful that the withdrawal of touch can be very powerful as well. "I'm going to take my hand away and go back to my chair. Tell me when you are ready." Follow that with, "Notice what happens when I take my hand away."

n. Process with the client and track their experiences.

o. Again, only use touch for a specific reason in the context of a specific use of mindful tracking.

p. IF YOU DO NOT FEEL COMFORTABLE USING TOUCH UNDER ANY CIRCUMSTANCE, you can use other methods to accomplish similar things. These methods include:

   1. Have the client imagine your hand on their hand, or imagine the hand of a loved one on their hand.

   2. Use something between you and the client such as a blanket or a pillow. If a client is holding their stomach, you can press a pillow against their stomach.

q. Document in your notes how touch was used during any session.

Chapter 19

Recognizing a Child State

As in many therapies, child states emerge frequently in the room. Working somatically with an attachment focus including the use of touch may somewhat increase the emergence of child states. Somatic attachment work specifically tracks the presence of a child state which can allow for more direct acknowledgment and focused attention in working with the child. Hakomi Psychotherapy, Sensorimotor Psychotherapy and Internal Family Systems work extensively with child states. Other therapies, particularly trauma treatments, might refer to this work as "parts work."

Working with a child state is an advanced skill. It takes time to learn to recognize the presence of the child and to work effectively. For the purposes of this workbook, it will be helpful just to start to recognize the signs of a child with this state emerging and to have some preliminary ideas how to work.

Signs of a child state:

    a. Mannerisms look younger: facial expression changes, head tilts, feet turn in.

    b. Voice changes: sounds younger, gets quieter.

    c. Content shifts: "I'm scared." "There's no one there."

    d. Energy shifts: gets quieter all-around, longer periods of silence.

e. Muscle changes: head and shoulders droop, pulled-in upper body, arms crossed.

f. You (as therapist) feel different: You feel more tender, more hesitant.

As a beginning Somatic Attachment Therapist, if you sense the presence of the child:

a. Seek confirmation: "Are you a little younger now?" "How old are you?"

b. "Where are you?" "Tell me what you are seeing."

c. Once you get a sense of what the child is experiencing, attempt to address it. Is she lonely? Is he frightened? Is there a traumatic activation?

d. For the most part, address a child state by talking directly to the child rather than to the adult. Your voice and word choices will change. Some clients will respond to the child being addressed directly while others may feel more comfortable if you establish the presence of the child part/state and ask to speak directly to the child part/state. At times, it may feel more appropriate to ask the client's adult self to communicate directly with the child. Track how your client responds as a guide to your next step.

e. If there is trauma being activated, move to resource by providing protection. "You're scared. I'm here to help you. Can you hear my voice?" "What if I came and got you?"

f. If there isn't trauma per se, talk from the heart to the child. "You're there all by yourself. I feel sad seeing you so alone. Can I come be with you?" "You know, sometimes adults just don't understand and they make mistakes. But I see you now and I'd like to be with you now."

g. Continue to track until something shifts.

h. Track closely as the person may move in and out of a child state.

In general, when working with the child, we are trying to provide a missing protective or nurturing experience that can begin to transform a traumatic or negative core belief.

Recognizing a Child State Exercise:

Let's go back again to Client 2 in previous chapters. It is written below as one vignette.

Client 2:

Her eyes are closed. Her mouth is set tightly and her jaw seems tense. She says in an agitated voice, "I notice a lot of thoughts, an image is coming up of my mother in her pajamas, she's pacing, maybe I'm four, I don't know, maybe we're in Fresno, oh, no, must be in Bakersfield by then, then we moved to Los Angeles, but that was later, the pajamas she's wearing are blue polka dot, I think, and her face is close to mine, she's saying something in a loud voice…"

She stops talking and becomes very quiet. Her body is still, her hands are held tightly against her sides, and her breathing is shallow. Her head starts to look toward the right and drops.

Write here three or more things you notice that might indicate she is in a child state:

1. _____

2. _____

3. _____

Write here a statement you could make to verify she is in a child state:

_____

Write here what you could say once she confirms she is in a child state:

_____

Write here how your delivery might change in speaking with her.

_____

_____

Write here what you see and hear that might suggest the client is dysregulated.

_____

_____

Write here what you might do to regulate the client if she is dysregulated.

_____

_____

Chapter 20

Meaning, Anchoring, and Integration (MAI)

I f a somatic session reaches completion, it will have led to a transformation of a core belief or a reinforcement of a resource. It is critical in either scenario to root the experience in the client's body and facilitate the integration into their everyday life. I have grouped these three skills together for ease of learning and remembering. They are concepts developed and utilized by the Hakomi Method.

Meaning usually takes the form of a positive statement of a previously-held negative core belief: "It's okay to speak up," "I will be safe if I speak up," "It's okay for me to rest," "I do have support in my life," "It's okay to accept help."

As the person's new belief emerges and is transformed during the session, have them repeat it and notice what comes up in the body. Deepen the person into that felt bodily or energetic experience.

Use whatever is identified as an *anchor*. To anchor, direct the client to notice if this a good place to hold this change. If so, direct them to deepen into it even further and to find a way to memorize the exact feeling. You can use a phrase like "Memorize this," "Imagine this as a tattoo," "Take this with you."

Integration is the final step in cementing the new belief in the client's mind-body experience. If possible, link back to the original story the client started with. "Imagine taking this with you as you spend time with your father next weekend. As you imagine that new belief and that sensation in your chest, notice how that feels." Then, deepen the client into it again.

Example of Meaning, Anchoring and Integration:

A client starts the session by talking about his anger that his father never seems to acknowledge what he does right. He feels belittled by his father and tends to be defensive when he is around him. He is going home for Thanksgiving and doesn't want to feel defensive or bad about himself. During the course of the session, the client's core belief, "I have to prove I am okay," transforms to "I am just fine the way I am."

Meaning

Therapist: So, just notice what happens in your body as your say that to yourself.

Deepening One

Client: The tension in my stomach is gone and I feel lighter in general.

Therapist: Okay, so let yourself feel the relief from the tension and that lightness.

Deepening One

Client: Yeah, feels good.

Therapist: Stay with that good feeling and let yourself feel it all over your body from the top of your head down through your toes.

Deepening One

Client: Yeah. (Body relaxing, smiling.) That really feels good. (Arms spread wide and relaxed on the couch.)

Therapist: Your arms are spread wide.   Contact Statement

Client: Yeah.

Therapist: Let's see if we can find the place in your body, or a movement or an energy that really captures this new belief, this good feeling. Does spreading your arms capture this new belief? Or, is there something else?

Anchoring

Client: Yeah, the arms spread and also an openness in my chest.

Therapist: So, let yourself feel into that openness and the spreading arms.

Deepening One

Client: Uh-huh.

Therapist: And, as you deepen into those sensations, just see if you can memorize them, how they feel, the expanse of your arms spread out, the breadth of that openness…

Anchoring

Client: Yeah…

Therapist: So, again, memorize these sensations and imagine taking them with you when you see your father next week.

Anchoring and Integration

Client: Yeah, I'm seeing him now and he's starting to go at me but my arms are spread and my chest is open, and you know what, these words just came up, "That's my father. It's not about me. I'm just fine the way I am." (Laughs)

Therapist: (laughing, too). How cool!   Contact Statement

Therapist: So, now, before you open your eyes and come back, is there anything else you want or need?   Transitioning

Client: No, this is great.

Meaning, Anchoring and Integration Exercise:

A client arrives at a new belief about her work life: "It's okay to slow down."

Write here how you would deepen into this new belief.

_____

The client puts her hand on her chest as you deepen.

Write here a contact statement and an anchoring statement

_____

_____

Write here what you might say to help the client integrate this new belief and somatic resource to take with her.

_____

_____

Chapter 21

Understanding and Working with Your Own Attachment Strategies

Considering Your Attachment Strategies

In Somatic Attachment Therapy, we are always monitoring the attachment bubble. In order to do that, we have to tune in to what is happening for us at any given point. Interactions with clients can cause some attachment dysregulation for us. This can be normal and often provides us information about what might be happening with the client. Learning to recognize what attachment responses we are having helps us to return to a secure place so we can remain present with the client and address the secondary attachment system of the client effectively.

Below are some ways to get a sense of how you tend to respond as a client and as a therapist. Take advantage of these tools in order to tune in to yourself emotionally and somatically in all aspects of your life.

1. The following link is an online attachment assessment tool that will indicate if you tend to react as "secure," "preoccupied," "dismissing," or "fearful-avoidant" (disorganized).

    http://www.web-research-design.net/cgi-bin/crq/crq.pl

2. Read the next set of statements to see which attachment issues surface for you a) as a client with your therapist and b) as a therapist with your clients. None of this is fixed: Read them with a view of what tends to happen rather than what always or never happens. The tendency/strategy noted in parentheses is likely accurate but will vary with the individual.

As a client with your therapist:

   a. I find it relatively easy to feel close to my therapist. (Secure)

   b. I do not worry about being abandoned by my therapist. (Secure)

   c. I find it difficult to allow myself to depend on my therapist. (Dismissing)

   d. Being vulnerable/exposed in therapy can make me feel weak or ashamed. (Dismissing)

   e. I find my therapist is reluctant to get as close as I would like. (Preoccupied)

   f. I am comfortable depending on my therapist within the clear limits of the therapist-client relationship. (Secure)

   g. I do not worry about my therapist getting too close to me. (Secure)

   h. I find my therapist is often not there when I need him/her. (Preoccupied)

   i. I am somewhat uncomfortable being close to my therapist. (Dismissing)

   j. It really bothers me that I feel more for my therapist than s/he feels for me. (Preoccupied)

   k. I know my therapist will be there when I need him/her as much as possible. (Secure)

   l. The therapist-client relationship boundaries bother me a lot. (Preoccupied)

   m. I don't like having to pay for my therapist to care about me. (Preoccupied)

   n. I get nervous when my therapist processes our relationship or issues between us during our session time. (Preoccupied)

o. I get resentful when my therapist processes our relationship or issues between us during our session time. (Dismissing)

p. I wish my therapist would focus less on my feelings and more on solving my problems. (Dismissing)

q. I trust my therapist really does care about me. (Secure)

r. I am sometimes scared when I am with my therapist. (Disorganized/Unresolved)

s. Sometimes I think my therapist will hurt me emotionally or physically. (Disorganized/Unresolved)

As a therapist with your clients:

a. I find it easy to feel close and connected to my clients. (Secure)

b. I do not often worry that I am not a good enough therapist. (Secure)

c. I find it difficult when clients depend on me. (Dismissing)

d. When clients express love or caring feelings for me, I tend to feel uncomfortable. (Dismissing)

e. I often feel good as a therapist that a client needs me. (Preoccupied)

f. When clients get angry with me, I often feel or am defensive. (Dismissing)

g. When clients are critical of me, I can usually listen and respond empathically. (Secure)

h. I have some fear of running into clients outside of therapy. (Preoccupied)

i. I often find myself stressed by a client's pain and suffering and believe the therapy is just not helping because of my skills. (Preoccupied)

j. When things get hard in therapy with a client, I often find myself wishing they would leave. (Dismissing)

k. When clients complain about having to pay me, the cost of therapy, or my cancellation policy, I tend to feel resentful and lose some empathy. (Dismissing)

l. Sometimes, if a client engages me in intellectual conversation about something in therapy, I can feel outmatched and bad about myself. (Preoccupied)

m. When clients leave therapy prematurely, I understand that it is not necessarily a reflection of my competence. (Secure)

n. In the world of therapists, I feel I am an equal amongst peers. (Secure)

o. When a client leaves therapy prematurely, I tend to label the client to explain it. (Dismissing)

p. Setting limits with clients is relatively straightforward and I can do it in a way that is empathic rather than harsh. (Secure)

q. I often find myself distressed by a session and spend a lot of time thinking and rethinking it. (Preoccupied)

r. When clients contact me a lot in between sessions, it is often hard for me to set a boundary. (Preoccupied)

s. Sometimes when clients get angry with me, I can become very scared. (Disorganized/Unresolved)

t. Often, I lose track of what is happening in a session and cannot remember what happened or what was said. (Disorganized/Unresolved)

u. Sometimes I feel hostile towards clients and don't understand why. (Disorganized/Unresolved)

Chapter 22

Working with Attachment in Therapy

Guidelines for Attachment In Therapy

1. Begin by understanding your own attachment strategies. Use the previous pages to get a sense of what happens for you with clients. What system do you tend to use when the work with a client becomes stressful?

2. Read the following seven statements by clients and note after each statement what your somatic and emotional responses are. Track yourself for hyperactivating or deactivating responses.

   a. "I'm sorry I called you so much last week but I was just so upset I really needed to talk to you."

   _____

   _____

   b. "It's irritating to me that we have to spend so much time talking about us. I want you to help me solve my problems."

   _____

   _____

c. "I can't stop what's happening in my mind – that scene just replays and replays and I am helpless, lying there, hurting, blood coming down my legs and my face almost numb from the pain …"

_____

_____

d. Phone message: "Hi, I can't come to therapy today. There's just too much stress and coming to therapy would just add to my stress – I need to take care of myself and just stay home. Besides I can't afford it today."

_____

_____

e. "YOU are the best, the greatest, like an earth angel."

_____

_____

f. "Interesting office. Reminds me of my first therapist's office. I couldn't stand him."

_____

_____

g. "I have been telling you and telling you and telling you and you just don't get it. I don't think you are such a good therapist for me. You keep getting it wrong and it pisses me off that I pay you to do a lousy job."

_____

_____

As you track yourself for your internal somatic and emotional responses as well as nervous system and attachment system activation, notice how you get yourself back into a secure place. Regulate yourself by utilizing WOT, resourcing, and your own internal community of attachment figures, including people in the therapeutic community who know your work and support you.

Below are the seven client statements again. This time, beneath each one write down what you did to return to a secure place and what that secure place feels like in your body.

h. "I'm sorry I called you so much last week but I was just so upset I really needed to talk to you."

_____

_____

i. "It's irritating to me that we have to spend so much time talking about us. I want you to help me solve my problem."

_____

_____

j. "I can't stop what's happening in my mind – that scene just replays and replays and I am helpless, lying there, hurting, blood coming down my legs and my face almost numb from the pain …"

_____

_____

k. (phone message) "Hi, I can't come to therapy today. There's just too much stress and coming to therapy would just add to my stress – I need to take care of myself and just stay home. Besides I can't afford it today."

_____

_____

l. "YOU are the best, the greatest, like an earth angel."

_____

m. "Interesting office. Reminds me of my first therapist's office. I couldn't stand him."

_____

_____

n. "I have been telling you and telling you and telling you and you just don't get it. I don't think you are such a good therapist for me. You keep getting it wrong and it pisses me off that I pay you to do a lousy job."

_____

_____

3. Pay attention to the "**Attachment Bubble**"

   a. Use your right brain to connect with the right brain of your client by sensing your client with your intuition, observation of client's movements, posture, eye contact, and moment-to-moment presence.

   b. Feel into your sense of being in the attachment bubble with the client. Do you feel connected, at ease, welcomed? Do you feel overwhelmed and needing some space? Do you feel distanced, not quite included, dispassionate by the same stories being told repeatedly even with intense emotion? Do you feel the bubble is slippery and scary, here and not here, making you worry about the client's safety and your own adequacy as a therapist?

   c. **If the bubble feels too crowded**, this could reflect a client's hyperactivating strategy. Look for the following somatic and content manifestations:
      1. Looser body stance
      2. Strongly inflected speech or rapid speech

3. Leaning forward posture
4. Possibly beseeching eye contact
5. More body movement
6. Client breathing more shallow, rapid
7. Irritation/anger with you
8. Emotional lability/intensity
9. Asking for your opinion/approval

Provide other-regulation through a calming voice, even voice inflection, and slower pace; use "we" language; self-regulate as needed; set necessary boundaries with compassion.

d. **If it feels like there isn't much of a bubble**, this could reflect a deactivating strategy. Look for the following somatic and content manifestations:

1. More rigid posture
2. Leaning back in chair
3. Slow breathing
4. Possibly flat speech
5. Spaciness, distractedness at times
6. Direct eye contact that might feel distant or averted eye contact
7. Repeated storytelling that doesn't feel present-moment even with intense emotion, leaving you feeling bored or dispassionate.
8. Chronically entertaining storytelling

Use playfulness and humor; look for ways to meet the client in terms of what they do well; self-regulate your feelings of disconnection to stay in contact; use a warm, engaged voice rather than a "warm and fuzzy" voice; look for places to connect in the moment and be secure as those moments fade.

e. **If the bubble is slippery**, pay attention to the active presence of significant dysregulation or disorganized attachment. Look for the following somatic and content manifestations:

1. Sense of hypervigilance
2. Eyes flitting back and forth
3. Intermittent eye contact
4. Body may be curled away
5. Dissociation
6. Client does not seem to feel safe or trusting
7. Verbally or nonverbally may move back and forth indicating desire to connect and fear of connecting
8. Content reflects chronic interpersonal fear/dysregulation

Bring the client back into the WOT and provide psychoeducation and practice with learning to self-regulate; work with the client to identify what makes them feel safe; articulate your desire for the client to feel safe; pay continuous attention to the client's level of safety with you; name what is happening; use your own dysregulation in the client's presence as indicator of the client's dysregulation.

4. For clients utilizing secondary systems, work over time to **establish the somatic footprint of a secure system**.

a. When have they felt secure before? What did it feel like in their bodies? What images go along with that?

b. Once the client has a clear physical and emotional memory of feeling secure, help the client move back and forth between the secure memory and an activated experience until the experience changes into something new and manageable, maybe even transformative.

5. **Be attuned to injury and proactive in providing repair and a return to safety**. Repairing present-moment attachment injuries is a crucial part of attachment work. Perfect is not possible nor desirable. Repair of an actual injury or a perception of an injury enhances trust and is key to developing a secure attachment.

Edward Tronick in a YouTube video, "Tronicks's Still Life Paradigm," states that the caregiver and child are only in perfect attunement 20% - 30% of the time. As therapists, we don't have to be in perfect attunement all of the time. Our percentage must be higher than parents, though, and we need to know how to do repair appropriately.

Sometimes repair will mean just a return to being present after "leaving" the client due to your own deactivating system. Sometimes repair will mean acknowledging you didn't understand the client at a crucial moment because you went into a hyperactivating system of "fixing the problem." Sometimes the repair will be a genuine apology.

Repairs must be done with attention to the current state of the client. If the client is in a child state, simply getting back the connection is the most important goal. Soothing for the emotional impact of the break may be the most appropriate course at first. Once the client returns to a more adult state, there may be room to understand how the break happened and draw connections with what happens for the client in their life. Repairs that are always apologies will not be helpful in the long term as the focus will be on what the therapist did wrong without understanding what strategies the client uses that may engender disconnections in the outside world.

Attachment Bubble and Repair Case Example:

Adela, an intelligent, articulate, charismatic woman in her early twenties, came to see me following an interview session with another therapist. Although she liked the other setting better, she chose to see me in part because of my positivity. In our first session, our conversation led me to say, "I start out with a respect and generic love for everyone." Over time, she let me know that generic love was not good enough for her: She wanted me to love her specially.

This theme played out in various ways over the course of our work together. Her need to feel lovable and special permeated her relationships and her sense of self. Nothing seemed to fill this deep internal hunger for feeling loved. Rather, she saw herself as a "brat," "a pill people needed to swallow," language used by her mother. As a result, she tended to push people who did love her, blurting out things semi-unconsciously to antagonize them into having an emotional response to her, and responding reactively to any sense of rejection. These ways of being with others were present with us and she was motivated and open to explore our interactions in search of her healing.

Her anxiety affected her ability to do general somatic tracking initially. However, we worked effectively to somatically regulate her in session and in relationships with friends. She began to see and experience her dysregulation in the moment with others and became increasingly successful in altering her behaviors.

Experiences of success in her general life and a sense of more control of her emotions and reactions calmed her down significantly. Intimate relationships, however, still dysregulated her intensely, leaving her with a sense of hopelessness and despair.

We were able to move more intensively into somatic tracking specifically around her difficulty absorbing the love that was available and building an internal sense of being lovable. We spent a few sessions experimenting with eyegazing which were dramatic in revealing her present-moment hyperactivated system, increasing her attach-

ment regulation, and building enough security to absorb my love and caring for her.

Adela had been living in hyperactivation most of her life. Early experiences did not create for her a sense that her stress, terror, sadness or fear would be attended to consistently. She was stuck in a cycle of reaching out to an available other she chronically experienced as not being enough, not being able to soothe her. My work became focused on being an available other: I sought to be present and consistent regardless of how she attempted in various unconscious ways to prove she was special and to test that specialness by behaving in ways that pushed me away.

In my years of practice, my own attachment strategies have moved from deactivating to hyperactivating to largely secure. In my practice, I noticed that, when stressed, I tended to fall into a hyperactivating system before righting myself. Some of the behaviors that reflected my preoccupation at times included going over time, at times accepting lower fees than I needed to, and being very flexible about people paying late, forgetting checks, or my doing all the billing work. These are not necessarily always a result of hyperactivation but I became aware that, at times, my anxiety about hurting someone or making them angry or upset led me to not take care of myself or address them directly with clients as part of the attachment dynamic.

These behaviors of mine were sometimes operative in my relationship with Adela. We were in the attachment bubble most of the time and I hesitated to lose the bubble by asserting something that bothered me: her not consistently paying me her co-pay at each session.

This hesitation had its consequences one day during the period of time when we were doing eyegazing. Just prior to session, I had received another notification from her insurance company that they were not paying for 5 sessions. I had dealt with the company previously about these sessions and was very frustrated when I received the notice.

I walked into the room with the notice in my hand. Adela came in exuberantly, "Oh, I forgot my check again today." My face was tight and my voice tense as I blurted out, *"Anthem is not paying for those five sessions and now you don't have your check."* Her face collapsed and fear immediately crept in. I could see her change and become younger before my eyes but was still dysregulated myself --- the hyperactivating system of not asserting myself for fear of reaction now became harsh interpretation. I said, less angry but still tensely, *"You didn't bring a check which has happened before. I wonder if this is a way to get me to take care of you, prove that you are special."*

She was upset and moved back and forth between the hurt and taking on my interpretation. *"I don't know – maybe I do want you take care of me. Maybe that's my brat part."* Her hyperactivating system was in gear. How could she appease me, get comfort from me when I was clearly upset with her? Her available other was turning out to be inconsistently available.

Right away, my insides melted. Her hurt and her fear shot through me and I was filled with regret for my tone and my aggressiveness. I had returned to a secure place and was able to reassert the attachment bubble with repair. I said, *"I'm sorry. I can see you are really upset. My frustration came out too harshly."*

She started to cry and I just let us both be there together with her hurt and my true regret. After a few minutes, I checked in with her in a soft voice,

Therapist: What's happening now, Adela?

Adela: I was thinking about the time we talked about my wanting to be held by you.

Therapist: Are you wanting that right now?

She looked at me and nodded.

I immediately went over and sat down next to her, still articulating the need for safety. *"Tell me what would feel right for you? It's important that you let me know if anything doesn't feel right, and I will be tracking closely to make sure you are safe."*

She told me exactly what would feel right and I held her as her body became wracked with sobs which continued for a long time. As I held her while she cried, I could physically feel her nervous system changing with the release -- slowing down, set-

tling in. Holding her became her path to safety. A lifetime of reaching for another and not feeling nourished or protected suddenly shifted. In her words, "You were upset with me and it was scary but I could see the 'sorry' in your face. That experience of being a 'brat' transformed to feeling loved despite doing something wrong."

The activation of a secondary system for each of us brought us to a moment of necessary repair. And, it was the repair that catapulted the work into the most significant transformation. Annoyance with myself for my frustration changed from regret to happiness – this attachment "enactment" led to the most meaningful change for Adela and an important tender landmark in our relationship.

Post-Test: Disorganized Attachment and Working with Attachment in Therapy

1. What is the primary indicator of a disorganized attachment:
    a. Lack of organization in daily life
    b. Fear/lack of trust
    c. Clingy behavior
    d. Devaluation of the therapist

2. What is the essential first goal of therapy for someone with a disorganized attachment:
    a. Establishing safety
    b. Increasing stability in everyday life
    c. Setting solid frame for therapy that accounts for unique needs of client
    d. All of the above

3. What phrase did Main and Hesse use to describe disorganized attachment?

4. If a client has a disorganized attachment, they do not use any secondary attachment systems. True _____ False _____

5. Of the following conditions young children face, which can result in a disorganized attachment?

    a. Severe depression of caregiver

    b. Inconsistent availability of caregiver

    c. Caregiver responses are harsh when child needs support/comfort

    d. Unresolved trauma or grief of caregiver

    e. Caregiver supports independence and toughness over contact and comfort

    f. Caregiver depends on child for own needs

    g. Early and prolonged separation from caregiver such as hospitalization

6. In working with attachment, what does it mean to pay attention to the "attachment bubble"?

    _____

    _____

7. Give an example of how your attachment tendency may interface with the attachment tendency of a client and help or hinder therapy.

    _____

    _____

Part IV:
Annotated Transcript and Vignettes

Chapter 23

Transcript of a Somatic Attachment Therapy Session

The following is a transcript of a demonstration conducted in a class I taught in August, 2013. We started out working in a non-somatic mode and then switched into a somatic attachment mode to elucidate some of the differences.

Non-Somatic Approach

Background: Client began by talking about a recent experience with some friends where the busyness of activity left her feeling invisible and as if there were no room for her. The session picks up about five minutes in:

Client: If someone told you something about themselves like that, wouldn't you ask about it, come back to it?

Therapist: Yeah.

Client: It's like, I don't know. (Shaking head)

Therapist: That seems hard. What was that like for you?

Client: It felt really strange. Like, am I invisible here? We're getting to know each other, then we are moving so fast, I'm off doing another task because this person is running so fast I can't keep up. I am just invisible.

Therapist: I imagine, given your background with your dad, this must have been really hard.

Client: Yeah, it was really hard but it was always like that. I had four kids in my family. So here is how I felt in my family….

Therapist: So how did that feel?

Client: I was really angry. Afterward I was walking along the street, and I thought I am going to stand up to her cuz she wasn't really listening to me, kind of like I am going to stand up for myself, stand up to you, that was really strange, not who I usually am, aggressive. I just stopped… (Rapid, somewhat truncated speech)

Therapist: What do you mean when you said you stopped? What was going on for you? What were you feeling?

Client: You are going to hear me, I said in my head (Voice strong, tense facial expression)

Therapist: In your head…So how are you feeling now as you are telling me?

Client: Kind of shy and kind of in it as I remember it. (Voice softer, eye contact slightly averted)

Therapist: Are you feeling shy with me?

Client: No, less shy, I am kind of angry,

Silence

Therapist: So who does this person remind you of?

Client: (Surprised, then thinking) My mother, oh, that is who she reminds me of.

Therapist: Your mother.

Client: My mom, I don't know, my mom was Beaver Cleaver mom, we were all busy, we were military, make community wherever we moved, had all these people over. We had to serve dinner to guests. One time we had to dress up as French maids. My mom and dad would make wine bottles with French labels and we would have guests sign the ceiling—was a big, big thing. I had to keep up with whatever was going on. I forgot about that. (Faster speech; surprise, some sense of "aha!" in remembering)

Therapist: Here you are having this experience last night, and then having this memory as a little kid where you had to serve everyone…

Client: You had to be really on, busy. I wasn't able to say anything, it was just expected.

Therapist: You couldn't speak up…

Client: Yeah, she was just telling me to move around, do this—I felt jerked around, and it's not my speed, she was really moving very fast, almost this out of control feeling.

Therapist: And that feels really familiar from your mom, being out of control, no place for you…

Client: I remember I couldn't be sad, I had to be happy, all of us together—ok, kids, all of you get in the car, I remember (Voice speeding up) she took all four of us and we are in the car going skiing, big old station wagon and we start sliding all over the cliff and the car was kind of teetering and she said, ok, kids, get on the tailgate. So we all get on the tailgate and she flags down these skier guys and they push the car back on the road and I am sitting on the tailgate trying to keep the car from going over and Mom is just, ok we will just figure this out. We got back in the car and continued down the mountain (Kind of laughing)

Therapist: So, no room for any of your feelings, fear…

Client: No, I forgot about that, what a trip, what a trip, that was weird. (Taken with the memory)

Therapist: You said you weren't allowed to be sad. Are you feeling sad right now?

Client: Yeah, a little sad.

Therapist: I can see that.

Client: The kids are scared but here we are off down the road again…

Therapist: Here you are in this scary situation…

Client: And we are off down the road again.

Therapist: Your mom is taking care of you but not protecting you or dealing with your emotions, nothing there for you emotionally...

Client: Yeah, and I was scared.

Therapist: I bet.

Client: I am thinking this is craziness sitting on the back of the car...

Therapist: It does sound crazy...How old were you?

Client: This is first or second grade, maybe 6 – 7, well, actually a little older, maybe 4th or 5th.

Therapist: I can't imagine what that was like, being so scared and not be allowed to show it.

Client: I always thought it was cool, I didn't know there was sadness, not fear, like skipping stones over the feelings.

Therapist: What if we don't skip stones today?

Client: Uhhh (Voice hesitant, eye contact slightly averted)

Therapist: Doesn't feel right? Can we stay with the sadness?

Client: Uhhh, I could try... (Hesitant)

Somatic Attachment Therapy Session with Annotation

(Continuing with the same session but switching therapeutic approach in working with the client.)

Note: The "client" in this session was an assistant teacher in the class, herself a therapist with significant somatic training. As such, she was already comfortable working this way and familiar with the method and the terminology. In order to have a session move this fluidly, a client in actual practice would need to give consent to working somatically, as well as to receive psychoeducation and a titrated introduction to working this way.

VERBAL AND NONVERBAL CONTENT	WHAT THE THERAPIST/CLIENT IS DOING
Therapist: So, are you feeling pretty comfortable right there?	Assessing acceptable physical proximity.
Client: Can you move here? *Therapist:* How is this distance here? *Client:* It's little far for me.	Speaking up for self/needs.
Therapist: Want me to move a little closer? *Client:* Yeah. *Therapist:* Is this better? *Client:* (Nods)	Permission-seeking.
Therapist: Good. So you just went through this experience in front of a lot of people you don't know very well...	Acknowledging impact of group context.
Client: What I am noticing is how racing I am inside. I am still racing... *Therapist:* Yeah. *Client:* Something right here, (Touching solar plexus), like a gerbil.	In touch with internal experience, dysregulation.
Therapist: Like a gerbil, you're making a gesture. (Hands cycling in air in front of body). Would you want to slow that down or just stay with it? *Client:* I will try. (Slows it down). No, it needs to stay faster.	Contact statement, deepening one. (Therapist does motion with client.)
Therapist: Needs to stay faster. Just let that happen, you're actually laughing as you say that.	Contact statement, deepening one, contact statement, supporting "defense."
(Both laughing) *Client:* I am having this amped up thing about the car over the edge, realizing, wow...	Nonverbal contact.
Therapist: Car over the edge... *Client:* Realizing, like wow--	Contact statement.
Therapist: Your body is remembering. Wow, is it ok to stay with it, you let me know if you have enough tolerance...	Contact statement, permission-seeking, assessing for level of regulation (Window of Tolerance).
Client: I'm fine, mid-upper range.	Regulated enough – can be in experience and observe at same time.
Therapist: Okay, good, just wanted to check in.	Asserting therapist will monitor for regulation.

Client: I am really curious, just curious.	
(Both laughing)	Nonverbal contact.
Therapist: You're really curious.	Contact Statement.
(Both laughing)	Nonverbal contact.
Therapist: This is big, having this memory…	Tracking with a "meaning" contact statement.
Client: This is really big, having this memory come back.	Affirms contact statement accurate.
Therapist: Surprising…	Contact statement from tracking emotion.
Client: Surprising, like it came out of nowhere…	
Therapist: What are you noticing as you are doing this? (Hand motions are continuing to go fast.)	Deepening one.
Client: I really like that you are doing this with me, the same movement. I can close my eyes or not, feels good, can connect with you or not.	Attachment safety; first glimpse in somatic session of possible insecure attachment system.
Therapist: Absolutely, feel free to do that. How do you know it feels good?	Invitation to safety and curiosity.
Client: I am laughing.	Nonverbal contact.
(Both laughing)	
Client: I am here with this big experience…	
Therapist: Yeah…	
Client: I'm laughing, the speed-up is there but it feels safe.	
Therapist: Feels safe	Contact statement.
Client: Let's both of us speed up, I know it's safe…Maybe that's the tires, I wonder. (Group: "Ohhhh…")	
Therapist: The tires going…	Contact statement.
Client: That's the image that came up, they are going fast, I notice my hands, too. (Moving in circular motion quickly)	
Therapist: I could feel that too as you said that,	Contact statement, joining.
Client: Trying to back up, but spinning…	
Therapist: So what's happening with those tires right now?	Deepening one.

Client: They need to get some traction.	Regulation desire; path to safety desire.
Therapist: While you are saying that, is there some image or sensation in your body? *Client:* There's a calming (Breath and hand motions slowing down).	Deepening one.
Therapist: Calming, okay, you slowed down a little bit...How do you notice feeling that calm? *Client:* I still have the speed in my solar plexus but the calm is still around me, shape of an egg is the calm part, but the inside part is the tires.	Contact statement and deepening one.
Therapist: Oh, if I do this, you kind of did this, (Imitating client's motion of hands held close together in "egg" shape in front of her body.) *Client:* I need to keep doing this.	Contact statement.
Therapist: Do the tires need to -- do you want me to do this movement with you?	Permission-seeking.
Client: I don't know, let's try both.....	Assessing need for support, possible deactivating system.
Client: Let's try me doing it then I'll stop, just notice. Ah, I just had a sense of aloneness.	Attachment dysregulation emerges more; awareness of need for connection in present time and in memory.
Therapist: I see that, thank you for telling me.	Appreciation for willingness to share vulnerability, acknowledge need.
Therapist: (Both laughing – therapist starts moving hands again) Now I'm going faster, you have me with you, you lost me for a second, now you have me back here with you. Notice how that is to have me— *Client:* It's cool. I have someone with me in that experience.	Gentle attachment exploration.
Therapist: Yeah, that's how it feels. I'm really glad to be here with you.	Affirming safety and mutuality of connection.
Client: I feel like I can let my tires stop. They are getting tired. (Both laughing)	Wave of traumatic activation completes; safety accompanies support/connection. Nonverbal contact.

Therapist: Tires getting tired and your hands dropped. Something shifted... *Client:* Yeah, there's a difference. Um, something inside shifted...	Contact statement.
Therapist: Something here shifted, and I sense some feelings came up, too.	Contact statement, emotional tracking.
Client: What the shift is, I'm okay and I'm not alone.	Attachment resourcing, meaning emerging.
Therapist: How beautiful, I am okay and not alone....What do you notice as you say that?	Contact and deepening one.
Client: I notice I am still bracing here.	Another trauma activation wave starts.
Therapist: So one part is feeling "I am okay, I'm not alone," but your body is still feeling being in that car. Is it ok to stay with that tension, just notice if there is any movement, micromovement, energy that wants to happen here?	Seeking completion of traumatic somatic activation.
Client: Umm, what wants to happen, I want to relax my legs, they were working pretty hard (Opens legs up wide, lets tension release)	Somatic wave starting to complete.
Therapist: They were, can I do that with you? Is that ok .....What do you notice when you relax your legs? *Client:* What a relief...	Permission-seeking, deepening one.
Therapist: What a relief, yeah, just let yourself feel that shift from tension to relief. Now you are crossing your legs...	Encouraging resourcing, contact statement.
Client: Still a little tension here...This side here.	Possible third wave starts.
Therapist: Does that side need anything, any movement need to happen there? *Client:* I think it needs to pull in more, feels like it has to come, like that. Client points to her outer thigh.That feels a little better.	Assessing need for further SNS completion, return to Window of Tolerance.
Therapist: That feels better. So, you made that shift, what did you notice? You said it felt better...	Contact statement, deepening one.
Client: I noticed a sense of more safety but, okay, I'm feeling I still need some protection, on guard, I can't go all the way to relax. I need to be safe.	Somatic traumatic memory needs more completion; possible deactivating system.

Therapist: You need some protection - can't go all the way to relax, need something in between…I'm going to ask you, feel free to say no, what if I came and put my hand there to help you feel safe, feel support? *Client:* Okay.	Deepening two – hunch connection through physical support will bring forward more attachment or regulation material.
Therapist: (Moving toward client) So, I am going to come forward and put my hand on your hand. Let me know if it doesn't feel right with me touching you. I am going to put my hand there, is that all right? *Client:* Yeah.	Use of touch, permission-seeking, tracking and contacting for impact and safety.
Therapist: How does the pressure feel? *Client:* Push a little harder…	Getting it exactly right.
Therapist: (Adding more pressure to her hand) What happened? *Client:* I just relaxed, there's still some tension on the inside…	Deepening one.
Therapist: Do you want to move your hand? *Client:* I think I need to stay this way.	Getting it exactly right.
Therapist: There's something wise telling you to stay this way. *Client:* This is good for now.	Affirming wisdom of body.
Therapist: Good for now. *Client:* Just put a little more pressure there…. This really helped. I just let the inside of my thigh relax.	Contact statement.
Therapist: Ok, just let yourself feel that relaxed feeling, just let yourself feel as much as you can. (Both laughing)	Deepening one with bite-sizing good feeling. Nonverbal contact.
Client: Feels good…..Comical, that story is so comical.	Resources self with humor.
Therapist: There *is* something funny about that story.	Contact statement.
Client: It's morphed, just a little bit of tension but not a lot.	Another minor wave.

Therapist: So just stay here a little bit, noticing what is going on with the tension. Is there anything else you are needing right now?	Deepening one.
Client: I think I need you not to touch me anymore.	Deactivating system, possibly in reaction to asking if she needed something.
Therapist: Ok, so just direct me how to take my hands away. Or should I just take them away? *Client:* Take this one first.	Immediate response to request for no touch but careful to get client's feedback how to withdraw touch.
Therapist: Like that? Let me know how it is to have my hands gone.	Assessing impact of withdrawing touch.
Client: I'm noticing how long I could have contact.	Awareness of attachment dysregulation, learning about self.
Therapist: Feels good to be able to have it that long, is that what you mean?	Clarifying, misunderstands meaning.
Client: Actually, the other, wow, <u>this</u> is the amount of contact I allow. Feels short, maybe that is my interpretation, and there's some sadness...	Processing presence of support, withdrawal of support.
Therapist: I want to be sure I understand – you had contact a shorter period of time than you would have –	Possible deactivating system for therapist in this moment in reaction to request by client to move away.
Client: Than I should have. I should have been able to have contact longer. So, I noticed when you pulled away, why am I asking you to leave? I didn't want you to leave.	Tender moment, felt experience of her own attachment dysregulation, deactivating tendency.
Therapist: You didn't want me to leave so now you are feeling sad, you didn't want me to leave...So now you're feeling sad, asked me to leave, didn't want me to. What would feel right, right now? Feel the sadness, or experiment with my touching, then pulling away (Somewhat speeded up).	Contact, back to secure system, offering choice .
Client: What seems right, this hand needs to be let alone, and this still needs to be there but I would like you to put pressure on there.	Asking for contact/path to safety.
Therapist: Ok. (Therapist places hand on client's hand again and applies pressure.) *Client:* Yeah, more pressure if you can.	Getting it right, Supporting the wisdom of working with her defenses rather than against.

Therapist: So, this is important…How much touch and contact you can have. *Client:* When you increased the pressure, I felt calm.	Contact statement, attempt at meaning.
Therapist: Can you stay with the calm, is that ok?	Permission-seeking given attachment dysregulation, deepening one.
Client: I am actually noticing the pressure, when you push in, it's telling me someone's really there with you. Someone's really there with me.	Letting herself accept/feel contact.
Therapist: So, just let yourself feel me really being there with you. *Client:* The pressure increases my calm. Silence. *Client:* That's good.	Attachment joining by changing "someone" to "me," deepening one.
Therapist: This having contact with each other, how does that feel to you?	Deepening one, asserting mutual contact rather than just her contact with therapist, affirming path to safety; is she safe enough to connect directly with therapist?
Client: Kind of fun, there's a lightness.	More able to stay with connection, feel the safety.
Therapist: Curious if there are any words at all?	Seeking meaning.
Client: It's not so hard to not be alone.	Beginning transformation of belief.
Therapist: It's not so hard to not be alone. Do you want to keep the words like that? *Client:* It's not so hard to not be alone.	Verifying right phrasing of new belief.
Therapist: So can you say it aloud and see what it feels like?	Deepening one.
Client: It's not so hard to not be alone	Meaning.
Therapist: Yeah, is there any place in your body that holds it? *Client:* I notice my voice, something came up, there's like an energy shift. (Hand coming out from her core towards therapist.)	Seeking anchoring.
Therapist: So let's notice that, there's a movement coming forward…	Contact statement, deepening one.

Client: There's something telling me, it's ok to reach out.	New meaning/belief emerging.
Therapist: It's ok to reach out. ..Now your hand is going out further. Does that feel like it's holding the somatic representation of that? *Client:* Yeah	Contact statement, seeking anchoring.
Therapist: So, we are going to bring this to a close in a little bit. Is this the movement you want to take with you?	Moving towards closure given time and emergence of transforming belief.
Client: Yeah, this is good, the reaching...	
Therapist: Ok, imagine taking this with you.	Somatically anchoring new belief; seeking integration.
Client: Ohh, it's okay to reach out and it's not asking for a handout.	Refinement of belief in line with lessening attachment dysregulation.
Therapist: Wow. Beautiful! It's okay to reach out and it's not asking for a handout.	Authentic joining.
Therapist: A few more things before we come back, you are doing this in front of a group of people even though we are pretty much in the bubble. Is there anything you need from the group?	Acknowledgment of present context, possible impact on attachment bubble; transitioning.
Client: I feel good. I feel excited and this is really fun for me.	
Therapist: Is there anything you need from me before we start discussing what happened?	Transitioning.
Client: I don't need your handouts. (Everyone laughing) *Therapist:* (Laughing) This is not a handout! (Everyone laughing)	Humorous reflection on change with lessened, but still present, attachment insecurity. Words, "need from me," may have triggered mild deactivating system. Feels a little surprised and a little pushed away but able to stay secure and respond by joining with her humor.

Analysis

The first session lasted approximately 10 minutes, the second 15 minutes. Even though both were abbreviated sessions for demonstration purposes, each was productive and led to the uncovering of key core beliefs. The first session verbally and with the use of insight kept moving her to make connections of present beliefs about herself with childhood attachment experiences. I was present and attuned to the story, the emotions, and the emergence of a discrete trauma memory. My voice is warm and she responds with increasing depth to emotional/insight explorations.

Core beliefs of "I am invisible" and "There is no room for me" emerge quickly. Two other beliefs emerge as the trauma memory surfaces: "It is not safe to feel" and "I will not be met emotionally." Whereas she states the first two beliefs, the last two are not articulated specifically. There is an awareness that feelings are skipped over but that awareness does not consciously get connected to her internalized messages. The session ends with my suggesting we not skip over the feelings today. She responds with hesitancy reflecting a defense against feeling which I catch but do not support. I ask again if we can stay with the sadness and she says she will comply but clearly does not want to.

There are various non-somatic responses to this situation that could have been used if the session continued. An intervention I might have used previously would have been to talk about her hesitancy and what she was afraid of. Again, this could have been effective in her learning more about herself and possibly having insight that, even though she wants her feelings attended to, there is a conflict for her when that attention is actually available. Good attachment work could happen out of this process over a longer period of time. It is likely, however, that the trauma memory will either not be processed or might take more time as my focus was on her feelings rather than on the totality of her memory including the somatic activation.

The second session starts where the first one ends. I initially check in to see how close she wants to be physically, sending the message that we will work within her comfort zone and only with her permission. It is obvious to me and to her that there has been a lot happening somatically and emotionally that the first session did not catch. She is somatically self-aware and starts out right away with a report of what's happening. The trauma memory is with her and she has already been experiencing some dysregulation. I check in early to make sure she is enough in the Window of Tolerance. As she is familiar with this concept, she is able to assert her ability to continue without needing resourcing. Her dysregulation level is there but contained enough for us to work on the traumatic activation. If there were no activation, we could not process the trauma.

She finds herself doing a motion that I contact and then join her in doing. It is my tendency to "accompany" people as they are doing motions and gestures. Later in this session, this "accompanying" leads to a more-clearly stated attachment conflict (deactivating system). As we work, we move back and forth between waves of somatic activation that complete and then settle and the live, felt experience of attachment dysregulation that is embedded in the trauma memory. She likes my doing the motion with her and reflects on the fact that she can connect with me or not. In general, this recognition of her choice would suggest attachment security. However, given what I know and have implicitly experienced already from the previous session, I am sensing a deactivating (dismissing) system emerging. The need and/or desire to connect is often fraught with fear and shame, and therefore it feels safer to disconnect.

In addition to doing some trauma resolution work, she has been able to work with these attachment beliefs and attachment dysregulation in real time. She gets to observe how she wants contact but pulls away and then experiences the loneliness. In this environment, all of this is available for observation and to be felt somatically as she finds the path to safety and secure attachment. Within the context of this session, she can allow herself to have a need/desire for contact, feel, explore, and be curious about the reticence that engenders, and try out a new belief.

The difference between the two sessions is what is allowed to surface and be worked on in real time. The first approach, though quite useful, is slower and, as of the point where it left off, does not offer a full emotional-somatic-cognitive integration. The somatic session, in contrast, allows for such integration as the left-brain neocortex understands what is transpiring while the right brain is experiencing it directly. An opportunity for transformation has opened.

Finally, the second session also demonstrates the use of the attachment bubble: I am tracking for a secondary attachment system in her and in myself, making choices that bear in mind what is needed in the moment that will increase her security. The emergence of the deactivating system at the end of the first session and in the second session leads me to actively connect with her humor and to minimize how "warm and fuzzy" I am. (These are semi-conscious decisions I became aware of only after reviewing the tape). I am maintaining warmth and at the same time monitoring for the possible emergence of shame when vulnerability and needs surface.

At the same time, I am tracking for any dysregulation in myself so that I can get back into the bubble as soon as possible. I believe some deactivating system came up for me as she asked me to remove touch and at the very end but was able to get back on track as I followed her, respecting her process and her felt sense of what she needed.

Chapter 24

Vignettes

This chapter offers two vignettes from seasoned therapists who work with a somatic attachment approach. Rebecca Silverstein describes an extended therapy with a client whose life experiences have led to a more deactivated mode of being in relationship. Alissa Blackman's work demonstrates a shorter-term therapy with a client with significant familial and community trauma whose internal process is a mix of avoidance and disorganization. Pay particular attention to the skillful manner each therapist uses in transforming awareness of her own somatic attachment reactions into creative and authentic contact with her client.

1. Teresa

By Rebecca Silverstein, MFT

TERESA, a 35-year old Latina lesbian, came to therapy to work on her problems with intimacy. She described herself as shy and a loner for much of her life. She wanted a partner but had never been able to sustain a relationship beyond a year. Teresa grew up in a big city in Texas with a violent father and a mother who was depressed, emotionally unavailable and passive. She moved away to attend college and since then has had minimal contact with her family. When Teresa came out as a lesbian in her early 20s, her parents were unsupportive.

As a result of a childhood where there was no one available for her to safely attach, Teresa learned early on to rely on herself and keep her relational needs out of her awareness. This avoidant or dismissive attachment style was evident in her history of leaving relationships abruptly, and of being attracted to distant, unavailable women.

Teresa was guarded in our initial therapy sessions but we established a good working relationship. I made a point of being especially welcoming, expressive and warm with her, finding places to inject some humor, which broke up her somewhat grave presentation. She spoke slowly and haltingly, as if it was an effort to get the words out. She usually looked down at the floor when talking, with occasional quick glances at me without making eye contact. She was short, muscular and compact, and I could sense the tension she held in her body.

Annotation: *Rebecca is describing effective choices she made to work with someone who presents predominantly with an avoidant attachment. Teresa is "wisely" guarded as a survival resource, unconsciously and limbically-activated to protect herself from being too vulnerable. Rebecca's warm presence coupled with humor allows Teresa to dilute some of the intensity and fear that would naturally accompany her seeking help and valuing her own needs and experiences.*

I had tender, warm and open feelings towards Teresa, yet I also felt very careful about not intruding in her space. This showed up in my body as tightness in my midsection and a feeling of pulling my energy inward. Teresa didn't express a lot of emotion when talking about her difficult childhood or her relationship history. I noticed that I pulled my energy in more while she related these painful stories. I seemed to be having a "mirror neuron" response to the way she walled herself off emotionally from both her pain and her needs for comfort and connection with me. This gave me somatic information on how she regulated. In those moments, I felt I was slightly dysregulated. I grounded myself by bringing my attention to my feet on the floor, and breathed into my diaphragm to loosen the constriction there. I visualized expanding my energy to fill up the room and surround her very gently. This allowed me to reconnect with Teresa in a way that didn't feel intrusive.

Annotation: *Here Rebecca is making excellent use of the "Attachment Bubble" by sensing into her own deactivating attachment response to Teresa in her own body. Consciousness of this enables Rebecca to bring herself back into a secure place so she can remain available as an attachment figure while allowing Teresa to stay safe.*

During a session about six months into the therapy, Teresa made a remark about the "butch/femme" dynamic among lesbians. I responded in a relaxed tone of voice about being a "femme" myself. I was taking a risk in teasing her a little and also acknowledging something about myself. I could feel the way this resonated for both of us in relating as two lesbians in that moment. She later told me how deeply significant this was, that she felt she was accepted and understood by me for the "butch" she was. She shared stories of being humiliated by her parents for not being a "girly girl" in the way she was expected to be in her Mexican, and Texan, culture. When I responded with deep empathy to these stories, she allowed herself to trust me and become more attached. This contrast to how unseen and unsupported she had been by her parents brought up strong feelings of what she had missed from them.

Annotation: *Rebecca's carefully-chosen use of self-disclosure coupled with the teasing demonstrates the developing connection between them and the increased safety for Teresa. Had Rebecca not responded warmly and acceptingly with contingent communication (adding a bit of herself in her response), Teresa might have felt shame, another element in an avoidant style.*

When Teresa was able to feel her longing for intimacy, she became more conscious of her awkwardness with others. I revealed that I had also battled shyness, which helped her feel she wasn't the only person with this struggle. I brought her awareness to moments when she felt connected to me and could feel me connected to her. We also worked somatically on her energetic boundaries. For example, I had her stand at one end of the room and notice in mindfulness what it felt like for me to move very slowly towards her from the other end of the room. We worked on the tension in her belly and the fears of rejection and hurt that lay beneath. This eventually led to some measure of relief from some of her muscular constriction.

Annotation: *As the relationship deepens, Teresa could let herself be vulnerable enough to work somatically. Rebecca contacts and tracks the somatic embodiment of Teresa's core belief, "I will be rejected if I allow myself to be close and vulnerable." Working together, they deepen her into the bodily sensations that protect her and experiment with choosing a different way.*

Teresa eventually began a serious relationship. She noticed how quickly her anger and withdrawal arose when her partner said something wounding. Through our work together, her own body awareness and acceptance of her feelings and needs grew. This allowed her to notice when she felt like withdrawing, and sometimes make the choice to stay present and talk when she felt hurt. Through the dynamics of her relationship, she could feel the impact of growing up in a family that hadn't "gotten" her on so many levels. She could understand why she still believed there was something deeply wrong with her and why she still feared that anyone she loved would inevitably abandon her. Over time, our relationship based on empathic attunement and deep connection helped her gain a stronger sense of her own worth and trust that she could be loved for herself.

Annotation: *Rebecca's somatic attachment work included her co-regulation of Teresa in session so that Teresa could experience safety finely-attuned for her needs, a fundamental aspect of attachment. Through co-regulation, Teresa learned to understand what her body was saying and to notice when she was in and out of the Window of Tolerance. The therapeutic process led to self-regulation based on an internalized sense of security cultivated lovingly by Rebecca.*

2. <u>Got Your Back</u>

By Alissa Blackman, MFT

ARTHUR, a 30 year-old, low-income Latino man, started coming to see me for PTSD treatment after his brother was shot just a few feet away from him. At the time he was struggling with painful intrusive memories of the incident, emotional numbness, depressed mood, and social isolation. He also suffered from panic attacks. This traumatic incident tapped painfully into Arthur's experiences in his family of origin. His parents were substance abusers: Daily neglect and lack of emotional/physical safety were prevalent for Arthur growing up. Arthur coped by developing fighting skills and living on the streets.

Although he grew into an overall calm, quiet person who avoided conflict, he also suffered from anger outbursts and hypervigilance. He preferred to avoid interacting with others outside the family, and occasionally his own kids' raucous play would evoke a startle response.

In exploring Arthur's past and present life to develop resources to support healing his PTSD, it became clear that he had lived much of his life on the edge without an expectation of safety or a "safe base." I viewed Arthur as having complex PTSD, a condition marked by developmental and attachment trauma, in addition to the discrete trauma of his brother's murder. Early on, it became clear that attachment work would be as important as more direct support for his recent trauma. We moved slowly, building trust and relationship.

Annotation: *Alissa's decision to move slowly was motivated by her intuition and awareness that trust and safety were key issues for Arthur. Community circumstances of violence were compounded by a family environment where he and his siblings were not kept safe. Chronic lack of interpersonal safety on the outside and in his home led to a vulnerability to affect dysregulation. In this case, Alissa clearly recognizes the attachment trauma that was an underpinning of Arthur's early life – no secure base, no predictability, no source of comfort. Individuals who experience terror with neglect* *may depend on a variety of attachment strategies unconsciously. Notice that she pays attention at any given moment to what attachment/dysregulation response is being activated as they work together.*

Many months into therapy, Arthur was speaking of his brother's death. In sharing these deep and vulnerable memories, he seemed stiff but was making an effort to bravely face his recent grief. As he spoke, he would pause, turn quiet and inward and then find more words. He started describing a song he'd heard that night with an ominous warning he did not heed. It was haunting him.

I felt a pull towards him to reach out and comfort, but I also sensed that I should keep my distance. I checked in to see if he was still "with me" in present time. At one point he reported feeling strange. My own perception of him had shifted so he seemed smaller, as if farther away. His face and posture looked fearful. After checking in, Arthur reported feeling a disorienting floating sensation. First asking if it was okay, I placed my sock-covered feet on his feet to ground him. His body relaxed and he looked me in the eyes again. With my feet on his, he could tolerate feeling embodied and present on the earth when grieving. Arthur felt relieved to be back "in the present moment," -- sad and angry, but also less terrified.

Annotation: *Alissa was monitoring for dysregulation by what she observed and what she sensed, utilizing her own nervous system as a guide. Notice that she seeks permission to use touch and then moves to resource him somatically. His ability to look her in the eyes again reflected his success in accessing the path to safety as an attachment resource. Alissa in that moment was co-regulating Arthur in a manner he did not receive as a child and possibly not as an adult.*

While Arthur felt he would benefit from "opening up" and feeling his emotions in order to heal, he felt too raw sensing his body and feeling his emotions, information he had "shut off" since his brother's death. Over time, alternating contact with our feet and introducing active somatic resourcing such as pressing his feet into the ground and tensing his thighs, doing wall push-ups, and squats, Arthur reported that he could feel his emotions in a less overwhelming way.

Annotation: *This is a beautiful example of titrating between hyperarousal and hypoarousal that accompanies trauma. Alissa is making sure Arthur is working at the edges of the Window of Tolerance so that he is not being re-traumatized. Doing this provides a sense of internal safety for him and helps him integrate vertically by noticing and working consciously with the reactions of the brain stem, limbic system and neocortex.*

In addition to supporting Arthur's emotional regulation around his trauma, it was clear that the use of touch in our sessions helped Arthur feel less alone in his grief. Our somatic work had grounded him to the earth and in relationship with me. Arthur tends towards a more disorganized attachment style leaning heavily on avoidant/dismissing survival techniques. He was able, however, to accept and feel nourished by negotiated contact without a lot of words. He reflected that he wasn't used to someone just sitting and being with him when he was sad. This comforted him and helped him feel safer while not having to take care of me.

Annotation: *Here is another example of attachment regulation during moments of overwhelm and terror. The experience of having Alissa monitor and hold safety for him is beginning to alter an early and frequently reinforced attachment belief, "I cannot trust or rely on anyone."*

One day Arthur arrived especially agitated. With angry words and elevated tone atypical for him in our sessions, he told me about an argument with his wife. While expressing satisfaction that he had walked away without lashing out, he remained activated by the event. He intensely shared the details of his story, pausing when I asserted verbal response, but scarcely registering me otherwise. He continued with the details of the fight, now speaking directly to me but as if speaking to his wife, "Now you call me out of my name? With all those people there?"

Arthur again appeared visually farther away to me in his chair. I sensed him spinning out of present-moment relationship. He was looking at me and speaking with me, but he seemed emotionally "back" in the incident and to be getting increasingly activated. His activation, coupled with his being out of mindfulness, led me to intervene directly. He needed to be regulated and embodied in order to go home safely.

Annotation: *Again, notice Alissa's description of Arthur's "spinning out of present-moment relationship." She wisely perceives through her own nervous system Arthur's activation and moves to bring him back into the present through somatic resourcing. Regardless of therapeutic approach, the re-enactment of the experience of trauma by itself is harmful to the client. In Somatic Attachment Therapy, following the client organically must be suspended in favor of immediate regulating through present-moment awareness. Somatic interventions are particularly critical at these moments as they represent dual awareness of the past and the literal present.*

I grounded myself quickly by turning my attention briefly to my sitting in my chair, grounding my feet. I subtly flexed my feet and leg muscles and took a big breath. I got ready to intervene more actively. "Okay," I said, diving in to the flow of words. "That was totally messed up and unfair. You feel so angry and hurt. And I totally get it. Of course! But let's also check how you're doing right now, while you're telling me this. What do you notice in your body?"

Annotation: *Alissa recognizes some slight hyperactivation in herself and takes active steps to move herself back to security. She grounds herself, contacts his feelings and the sense of betrayal, then focuses him somatically.*

He stopped then, tightening his jaw, turning his attention inside. After a time he said, "Man, I'm just getting angrier and angrier." When he stopped to notice, he said, he was tense in his shoulders and ready to fight.

"Ok," I said, "Can we slow this whole thing down?" He took a breath and agreed. "This is familiar isn't it?" I asked.

Annotation: *Notice the use of slowing and deepening two interventions.*

"Oh yeah," he said, shaking his head grimly and taking a breath, coming into broader awareness. "Oh, how familiar it is." His arms, bent at the elbows, hugged his torso more tightly for a moment and then hung from the shoulders, a bit stiff.

A memory surfaced for Arthur then — witnessing his father pistol-whipping his mother when he was five. He described the story slowly and matter-of-factly as though it had happened on television. I could feel inside me intolerable feelings of fear, helplessness and rage he was not then expressing.

I said, "Whew. You were only five. You really needed someone to have your back, huh?"

Annotation: *Through working with regulation and somatic experience, a core belief emerges that Alissa contacts: "There is no one to protect me." Take special note of how she physicalizes this for Arthur through metaphor, providing him with a corrective, transformative moment.*

"Got that right," he said looking at me and hunching forward slightly. His back body seemed armored and so powerfully protective in survival mode. He needed his power to be there for him and, at the same time, he was deep inside himself, protected but alone.

At this point, my heart was still resonating with his story as a five-year-old. There was something hanging in the air. I sensed something new that maybe wanted to happen. I asked if he'd like to see if using touch, specifically my actual hand on his back, would help him feel calmer and less alone. It sounded sort of "different," he said, but was willing to try. I asked him to check throughout his body to see if he felt comfortable. He said something relaxed in his chest when he thought about the idea.

Annotation: *Alissa is using a deepening two intervention based on her sense that* *something needed to happen. Attuned to attachment, she identifies the attachment belief through phrasing that deeply reflects his experience.*

"Okay. I am going to come next to your chair," I said. I got up and knelt next to his seat. "I will put my hand on your back, and you let me know how it feels. If anything about how I am touching you doesn't feel right or needs to change, you just let me know. Okay?" He agreed.

I stood and knelt to the left of his seat. I let him know I was ready to place my hand on his back and asked if he was ready. When he said he was, I placed my hand on the middle of his upper back, behind his heart. We sat together breathing, his back slowly allowing my hand to rest down more and more. Long moments passed. Gradually he breathed more deeply, and settled further back into the chair "How does this feel?" I asked.

Annotation: *As she works somatically, she is careful to track the impact of the use of touch, particularly important with clients who have been exposed to or were victims of physical/sexual abuse.*

After a moment he turned his head towards me. With a warm smile, he said, "Yeah, I am feeling better already. That is pretty strange. Really pretty strange."

"Yeah?" I said. "Strange?"

"Yes. A little like magic."

"Wow," I said. "Yeah, it is a bit like magic to feel a bit better so fast. Like an everyday person-to-person magic. What tells you that you are feeling better?"

"Well, I feel more easy inside. Like I landed in my chair." I could see his eyes were slightly wet. "Thanks, that really feels better. I don't want to be that way. How I was. It doesn't feel good." He sighed.

With permission to move my hand, I sat back across from him. Now he took a breath but did not exhale. "But, um, I don't want to get too calm. You know."

I felt a tension in my own body as he tensed ever so slightly.

"Something might happen?"

"Yes," he said. "Out there things happen." He looked out the window.

"Yes. Got it," I said. As good as it may have felt to be more relaxed, easy and open, understandably Arthur would want to leave the office feeling ready to face his daily life, a life very different from the therapy room. Truly "having his back" would mean offering an additional support resource.

"What do you think your body needs right now to feel safer?"

Annotation: *Alissa demonstrates a powerful awareness of the wisdom of defenses. She recognizes and actively honors Arthur's ongoing reality and need to protect himself in his current life.*

A long moment passed. Arthur looked at me with clear eyes. "I'm remembering when I used to box. I'd like to feel that way. Like I could knock you out cold, but I had, like, flow. I wasn't all… blocky like this."

The intervention with my hand on his back appeared to have shifted him to a para-sympathetic state, calming him, and slightly relaxing his chest. I sensed that activating the muscles in his front body could help him feel safer and balanced without disconnecting him from the "flow". He agreed to this idea.

After joining him in standing grounded, each with wide stances, I explained where my hands would be on the front of his shoulders and explained the movements we would explore. "Okay, swing your shoulders forward and in, like trying to touch your shoulder points in front of you." He swung his big shoulders forward against my hands, a resistance exercise. I suggested he now pull the points of his shoulder blades together in back, as if he had wings. He did so, and then pulled his front shoulders forward again. "I can feel it," he said. "This is good."

"How is it good?" I asked.

"Feels strong," he said. "But like, flexible."

After three repetitions, we stopped. "Okay, how does that feel now?"

He took a big breath and nodded, looking at me with a surprised smile. "Yeah, good.

Like, I feel, still a little angry of course, but like I have more space. I feel powerful but more calm. Like I can handle whatever."

Annotation: *Arthur's sense of his wife's betrayal, the trauma echoes of his brother's death, and his mother being pistol-whipped were able to shift through Alissa's in-the-moment somatic and attachment tracking, and his own courageous engagement with his process. He was able to leave with the somatic imprint of Alissa having his back now in his own body, able to be present and protect himself simultaneously.*

Part V:
Tying it All Together: Body, Brain, Love

Chapter 25

Body, Brain, Love

W hy name this book, *Body, Brain, Love*? Why not *Body, Brain, Security*? After all, attachment is usually described in terms of someone feeling secure or insecure rather than loved or not loved. I emphasize love because I believe it is the essential ingredient that underlies mental health and that therefore underlies our capacity to help our clients find or return to mental health.

In the field of psychotherapy, there is a legitimate and understandable moral and ethical concern about boundaries. Therapists are appropriately concerned that the focus of therapy be the client; we try with integrity to maintain these protective boundaries. As clinicians in the field, we are well aware of practitioners who, usually as a result of their own unconscious and unresolved attachment insecurity, do not retain sufficient boundaries with clients.

Our therapy association magazines regularly report disciplinary actions for therapists who have exploited clients sexually, financially, and emotionally. For good reason, we are apprehensive about doing the same. We are mindful that making ourselves emotionally available for our clients might engender a strong dependency or erotic transference or seemingly out of control feelings on our clients' parts. Some clinicians are fearful their own feelings might spiral out of control. Laws governing the practice of psychotherapy, as well as our examination and licensing processes, all stress these boundaries. And they should. For many years, there wasn't enough accountability and awareness. We needed to focus on and tighten boundary awareness.

For many clinicians, however, this notion of boundaries can be a source of anxiety, causing an unnecessary level of detachment from clients. The frame of the work has its own level of detachment built in. Clients often already feel a little distanced by the "rules" of therapy and what is/isn't appropriate. We know the frame is necessary on many levels for therapy to be effective: It creates the circumstances for a unitary focus on the best interests of the client; it offers predictability schedule-wise and financially for therapists; it helps maintain the quality of intensity and focus that underlies transference, counter-transference, and other critical factors in transformation; and it enables the "growing experience" of therapy—i.e., that clients do not live their lives in therapy but rather learn how to lives their lives through therapy.

And, a well-kept frame, I believe, still allows for love. There is a way to be engaged emotionally with clients, to feel deeply connected and deeply caring such that a real secure attachment is fostered and then internalized. Ultimately, Somatic Attachment Therapy works on this premise. Generic mindfulness (awareness of the impact of therapeutic interventions by the therapists) and client mindfulness (observation of and curiosity about internal experience) can assure boundaries and at the same time facilitate the two goals of Somatic Attachment Therapy: 1) an earned secure attachment, and 2) development of a coherent narrative. (Concept used in the Adult Attachment Interview).

When I was in training, one of my favorite supervisors told me, "Therapy is an education and an experience." We use mindfulness so clients can learn about and experience themselves completely. We approach with love so they can learn about and experience themselves in relationship.

In writing this chapter, I looked up the various kinds of love. I was assuming the love I meant was "agape." Agape, however, does not fit. It refers to a sacrificing, unconditional love for the divine. After reading through different definitions from various sources, the only phrase I could come up with that works is "attachment love." Although it is an awkward term, I think it captures the essence of the kind of love we as therapists need to have for our clients:

1. It alludes to the attachment process which is critical for infant emotional and physical survival.

2. It specifically excludes sexual love or friendship love.

3. It contains the necessary ingredients of protection, comfort, safety, availability, appropriate challenge, boundaries, and differentiation.

Attachment love, as suggested throughout this workbook, is a neurobiological necessity for survival. It is not a Pollyanna-type concept that glosses over reality. Rather, it is an evolutionary design. According to Rich Hanson in *Buddha's Brain*, mammal and bird brain development started around 180 million years ago. Unlike reptiles and fish, mammals and birds raise their young and therefore needed significantly more brain capacity and neural circuitry. Brain size and brain complexity increased to accommodate structures that facilitate attachment.

Brain wiring for attachment is something we share with all mammals. *In the Science of the Art of Psychotherapy*, Allan Schore writes with Gay Bradshaw about the eroding of attachment bonds in elephants in the wild. Culling (systematic killing), poaching, translocations, and other human-initiated actions have altered the social engagement behaviors of elephants within their communities. New realities such as absence of intact families, separations of the young from their parents, and premature weaning have all caused increased aggression, nonconsensual sex, poor mothering, and infant neglect, amongst other things. These elephants are as impacted by attachment disruptions as we are and their brains are altered by insecure attachment as are ours. (Schore, 2012, Chapter 7, pp. 243- 258.)

As attachment is neurobiologically wired in mammals and humans, so is love. They go hand in hand. Love is both the physiological mechanism for the development of a secure attachment and the outcome of a secure attachment. We need food, water, air, and shelter for life, i.e., literal physical survival; we need love to develop normally and to thrive physically, psychologically, mentally, and spiritually.

Given this physiological and brain-wired imperative in universal mental health, how can we as psychotherapists not consider love a central tenet? Good problem-solving therapy can happen without love but I do not believe true transformation can.

We know we use our own selves in our work. I believe that means using all of our human connectedness and capacity for love as well. As you digest the information in this workbook, consider how you can bring your full self forward in your work. You will be amazed.

Appendices

Appendix 1

Glossary

Somatic Attachment Therapy: Theory and practice of facilitating permanent physiological, psychological, and spiritual change in clients through the understanding and application of affect regulation and attachment regulation for both client and therapist.

Somatics: Theory and use of body-focused skills to track present experience and facilitate access to information stored in unconscious emotional and physical memory.

Didactic Neuroscience Material

- **Implicit Memory:** Physical and emotional memory originated and stored in brain structures that primarily function unconsciously.

- **Explicit Memory:** Memories that are available consciously and can be easily retrieved through language.

- **Regulation:** Homeostatic balance of the autonomic nervous system on a moment-to-moment basis that allows for response to everyday stresses in a present-moment manner.

- **Dysregulation:** An acute or chronic state of activation of different aspects of the autonomic nervous system in response to the perceived presence of threat or danger.

- **Secure Attachment:** Presence of an embodied sense of intrapersonal and interpersonal security that facilitates emotional and physical regulation.

- **Insecure Attachment:** Dysregulated states of mind that are activated emotionally and physically associated with interpersonal relationships or internal representations of past relationships with primary caregivers..

- **Autonomic Nervous System:** Electrical and neurochemical brain system comprised primarily of the sympathetic nervous system and the parasympathetic nervous system that instinctually and unconsciously attempts to protect us from threat or danger.

- **Reptilian Brain (Brain Stem):** Earliest, least-developed brain structure found in all animals. Brain of lizards, snakes, turtles. Driven by instinct, response to environmental threat.

- **Mammalian Brain (Limbic System):** Second layer of brain structure that covers reptilian brain in all mammals. Responsible for emotions, memory, learning and attachment.

- **Neo-Mammalian Brain (Neo-Cortex):** Third layer of brain structure which covers mammalian brain in humans only. Responsible for language, thought, analysis.

- **Sympathetic Nervous System:** Electrical system primarily housed in the limbic system which responds to brain stem and limbic system signals of threat in fight or flight mode. Also responsible for feelings of excitement, joy, and sexual pleasure without activation of fight/flight.

- **HPA-Axis:** Hypothalamus-Pituitary-Adrenal Axis which responds in tandem with the sympathetic nervous system to release necessary stress hormones of cortisol and epinephrine to mobilize in response to threat.

- **Parasympathetic Nervous System:** Branch of the autonomic nervous system which keeps the body in rest and digest mode or returns to homeostasis following sympathetic nervous system activation. Also responsible for drastic survival responses to extreme danger in the form of system shutdown, reduced respiration and heart rate, fainting, dissociation, freeze, and submit.

- **Vagus Nerve:** Tenth Cranial Nerve, part of the parasympathetic nervous system. Starts in the brain and continues through to major organs and muscles including heart, lungs, stomach. Has two significant components: ventral vagal complex and dorsal vagal complex.

- **Ventral Vagal Complex:** Action of the upper, newer, myelinated part of the vagus nerve which goes through the heart, facial muscles, and ear muscles to restore a sense of safety. The social engagement system which allows for a return to safety through comfort or play exists here.

- **Dorsal Vagal Complex:** Action of the lower, older, unmyelinated part of the Vagus Nerve which moves through the spinal cord to lower organs including the heart, lungs, and stomach to preserve survival under extreme danger by precipitating immediate bodily shutdown, freeze, and submit.

- **Thalamus:** Brain structure that sits atop the brain stem. It receives sensory information representing possible danger and sends the signal to the amygdala, hypothalamus, and hippocampus. Acts in nanoseconds outside of consciousness.

- **Amygdala:** Brain structure in the limbic system that receives the signal from the thalamus and rings the alarm bell to activate the sympathetic nervous system or parasympathetic nervous system depending on the degree of threat. Acts in nanoseconds outside of consciousness.

- **Hypothalamus:** Critical part of the HPA-Axis in the limbic system that receives the signal from the thalamus and activates the neurochemicals of epinephrine and cortisol to enable the body to respond in fight or flight mode. Acts in nanoseconds outside of consciousness.

- **Hippocampus:** Brain structure in the limbic system which receives the signal from the thalamus and amygdala to begin the slower neocortical process of evaluating the degree of the danger. Works in tandem with the amygdala and the neocortex.

- **Amygdala-Hippocampus Connection:** Very important synaptic and fiber connection that either allows for the presence of neocortical appraisal/thought or inhibits it. One physiological goal of therapy is to enhance the client's amygdala-hippocampus connection.

- **Hyperarousal:** Chronic or acute activation of the sympathetic nervous system reflecting fight-flight reactions.

- **Hypoarousal:** Chronic or acute activation of the parasympathetic nervous system reflecting freeze or submit reactions.

Therapist Concepts and Tools for Regulation

- **Window of Tolerance:** Central tool of the somatic attachment therapist's toolkit. Depicts three bands of experience the person could be having at any one moment and allows for a slow, body-based awareness to bring the person back into emotional and physiological regulation; state of nervous system experience that is calm and enables thinking and feeling at the same time in present-moment consciousness.

- **Resourcing:** Central tool of the somatic attachment therapist's toolkit; understanding the difference between survival, transitioning, and creative resources; using somatic, interpersonal, spiritual, and other resources to facilitate regulating clients and helping clients regulate themselves.

- **Other-regulation or Co-regulation:** The concept and practice of using the calm nervous system of the therapist to regulate the activation of the client through somatic and other resources including the attachment bubble.

- **Auto-regulation or Self-Regulation:** The concept and practice of the client regulating himself or herself through the use of transitioning and creative resources.

- **Attachment bubble:** Central tool of the somatic-attachment therapist's toolkit. Therapist awareness of and use of the concept of the bubble to assess and work with where the client and therapist exist in the therapeutic relationship at any given moment.

- **Survival resource:** A resource used, usually unconsciously, to protect someone from a sense of threat or danger, including the anxiety or terror associated with abandonment, abuse, or neglect. Examples include: substance abuse; cutting; isolation

- **Transitioning resource:** A resource used by someone as they become cognizant of the nature of a survival resource and they make a conscious choice to try something different. Examples include harm reduction en route to abstention; eating compulsively instead of drinking compulsively.

- **Creative resource:** A resource used by someone to manage stress and dysregulation that is newer, different, and essentially healthy and conscious by intention. Examples include mindfulness, meditation, group work

- **Hyperactivating Attachment System:** Nervous system and neurochemical responses to threats associated with an anxious/preoccupied attachment.

- **Deactivating Attachment System:** Nervous system and neurochemical responses to threats associated with an avoidant/dismissing attachment

Somatic Skills

- **Basic Somatic Skills:** Central tool in somatic attachment therapist's toolkit: mindfulness, tracking, contacting, slowing, deepening one and two, supporting the wisdom of defenses, recognizing a child state, meaning, anchoring, and integration.

- **Mindfulness:** slow, careful, moment-by-moment observation of internal experience with curiosity and without judgment.

- **Tracking:** Observation by the therapist of emotional, physical, and energetic aspects of the client's experience that are being manifested on a moment-by-moment basis.

- **Contacting:** Verbal and/or nonverbal direct naming to the client what the therapist has tracked.

- **Slowing:** Encouraging the client to slow down their process to gain a deeper, more nuanced sense of internal experience; skill used by therapist to regulate internal experience when activated by client's activation.

- **Deepening One:** Encouraging client to stay with an experience that has been contacted.

- **Deepening Two:** Interventions used to deepen client's experience based on therapist instinct or hunch.

- **MAI:** Trio of skills used to complete a session or reinforce a resource – "Meaning" (identifying new belief that has emerged); "Anchoring" (finding the somatic or energetic manifestation of that belief and anchoring it in the body); and "integration" (helping client take new belief back into their life.)

Bibliography

Badenoch, B. (2008). *Being a brain-wise therapist: A practical guide to interpersonal neurobiology*. New York: W.W. Norton & Company.

Badenoch, B. (2011). *The brain-savvy therapist's workbook*. New York: W.W. Norton & Company.

Buczynski, R., & Porges, S. (2012). *The polyvagal theory: Why this changes everything.* nicabm.com. Retrieved August 21, 2014 from http://files.nicabm.com/Trauma2012/Porges/NICABM-Porges-2012.pdf.

Cozolino, L. (2002). *The neuroscience of psychotherapy: Building and rebuilding the human brain*. New York: W.W. Norton & Company.

Creativity in early brain development. Date and author unknown. *earlyarts.co.uk*. Retrieved April 4, 2014 from http://earlyarts.co.uk/philosophy/creativity-early-brain-development/.

John Bowlby. *wikipedia.org*. Retrieved March 12, 2012 from http://en.wikipedia.org/wiki/John_Bowlby.

Dykema, R. (March/April 2006). How your nervous system sabotages your ability to relate: An interview with Stephen Porges about his polyvagal theory. *nexuspub.com*. Retrieved September 7, 2014 from www.nexuspub.com/articles_2006.

Fisher, J. (2007). *Psychoeducational aids for working with psychological trauma*. Cambridge, MA: Kendall Press.

Guldberg, H. (July 16, 2013). The deterministic myth of "The early years." spiked-online.com. Retrieved February 2, 2014 from http://www.spiked-online.com/newsite/article/infant_determinism/13814#.VFVjNfldWSo.

Hansen, R. & Mendius, R. (2009). *Buddha's brain: The practical neuroscience of happiness, love and wisdom.* Oakland, CA: New Harbinger Publications.

Karen, R. (February 11, 1990). Becoming attached; theatlantic.com. Retrieved August 29, 2014 from http://www.theatlantic.com/magazine/print/1990/02/becoming-attached/308966/.

Karen, R. (1999) *Becoming attached: First relationships and how they shape our capacity to love.* Oxford, UK: Oxford University Press.

Levonian, E. (2012). Tronick's still face paradigm. youtube.com. Retrieved January 12, 2013 from https://www.youtube.com/watch?v=bG89Qxw30BM.

Mayhem, A. (2010). Strange situation experiment.mp4. youtube.com. Retrieved January 12, 2013 from https://www.youtube.com/watch?v=PnFKaaOSPmk.

Mikulincer, M. & Shaver, P. (2007) *Attachment in adulthood: structure, dynamics and change.* New York: The Guilford Press.

Ogden, P, Minton, K. &Pain, C. (2006). *Trauma and the body: A sensorimotor approach to psychotherapy.* New York: W.W. Norton & Company.

Attachment theory vs temperament: Treating attachment disorder in adults. The evolution of the brain in humans: What therapists need to know. Somatic therapy; Using the mind-body connection to get results. (2012- 2014); *psychotherapynetworker.com.* Retrieved August 27, 2014 from http://daily.psychotherapynetworker.org/free-reports/.

Schore, A. (2012). *The science of the art of psychotherapy.* New York: W.W. Norton & Company.

Siegel, D. (2001) T*he developing mind: How relationships and the brain interact to shape who we are.* New York: The Guilford Press, 1st Edition.

Siegel, D. (2010). *Mindsight: The new science of personal transformation.* New York: Bantam Books.

Siegel, D. (2008). *The neurobiology of "we": How relationships, the mind and the brain interact to shape who we are.* Soundstrue.com. Sounds True Audio Learning Course.

Siegel, D. (2012). *Pocket guide to interpersonal neurobiology: An integrative handbook of the mind.* New York: W.W. Norton & Company.

Strange Situation. Wikipedia.org. Retrieved August 11, 2014 from http://en.wikipedia.org/wiki/Strange_situation.

Wilkinson, M. (2010). *Changing minds in therapy: Emotion, attachment, trauma and neurobiology.* New York: W.W. Norton & Company.

Resources: Where Do You Go From Here?

———————

After completing this workbook, you may want to continue learning how to incorporate the information or work into your practice. The following are resources for further training and reading.

- **Hakomi Psychotherapy:** www.hakomiinstitute.com

- **Sensorimotor Psychotherapy Institute:** www.sensorimotor.org

- **Accelerated Experiential Dynamic Psychotherapy (AEDP):** www.aedpinstitute.org

- **Somatic Experiencing:** www.traumahealing.com

- **Eye Movement Desensitization and Reprocessing:** www.emdr.com

- **Emotionally-Focused Therapy (EFT):** www.iceeft.com

- **Interpersonal Neurobiology Series by W.W.Norton and Company:** www.wwnorton.com

- **UCLA annual Interpersonal Neurobiology Conference:** www.uclaextension.edu or www.lifespanlearn.org

- **Focusing Therapy:** www.focusing.org

- **Somatic Attachment Training and experience (SATe):** www.dianepooleheller.com

- **Formative Psychotherapy:** www.centerpress.com

Answer Key

Chapter 4: Matching Game (page 22):

Answer Order: 7, 11, 8, 12, 5, 10, 9, 1, 2, 4, 6, 3

Chapter 4: Post-Test (page 23):

1. Reptilian/Brain stem; Mammalian; Neocortex/Neomammalian.

2. Reptilian—autonomic functions such as breathing; instinctive detection of threat/danger; Mammalian—emotions, memory, procedural learning, attachment; Neocortex—thinking, appraising, analysis, language.

3. Sympathetic—responds to threat/danger through fight or flight responses; Parasympathetic—responsible for "rest and digest," general homeostasis, social engagement.

4. The limbic system responds within nanoseconds; the neocortex responds more slowly as it appraises the situation.

5. The amygdala, in the limbic system of the mammalian brain, receives sensory information through the thalamus and activates the alarm system when danger is perceived.

6. The amygdala and hypothalamus activate an electrochemical response to danger by releasing cortisol and epinephrine and sending electrical signals to muscles and organs in the body. Fight or flight responses include dilated pupils, increased muscle tension, increased heart rate, shallow breathing,

increased flow of energy to the large muscles such as arms and legs, decreased digestion and immune system function.

7. The hippocampus receives a signal from the thalamus as does the amygdala. The amygdala responds immediately while the hippocampus sends the information to the middle prefrontal cortex for appraisal of the reality of danger. Once the determination is made that the danger is not real or serious, the hippocampus sends that information back to the amygdala to shut down sympathetic responses.

8. When the middle prefrontal cortex has the opportunity to respond and quiet the limbic system amygdala and hypothalamus activation, the parasympathetic nervous system restores the body to homeostasis, and "rest and digest "through another electrochemical response of oxytocin and acetylcholine.

9. Trauma interrupts the normal autonomic nervous system responses of sensing danger and responding to it, appraising and then recovering. With trauma, the amygdala and hypothalamus are chronically overwhelmed with information that the body is endangered and are therefore chronically activating an electrochemical response. The hippocampus, working much more slowly, cannot keep up with the pace and becomes overwhelmed. Everyday situations that are not dangerous are still perceived as such as there is inadequate assessment, appraisal, and opportunity for ANS recovery.

10. Regulate and integrate.

Chapter 5: Exercise (page 31):

1. Regulated. She is spaced out as many of us are during the course of a day but still well within the range of normal regulation.

2. Mildly and momentarily hyperaroused. Her body responds reflexively to an immediate danger but doesn't go into full hyperarousal once her neocortex

appraises and responds to the situation at hand.

3.   Regulated. Parasympathetic nervous system has brought her back to homeostasis.

4.   Hyperaroused. Her body responds to the immediate danger by sending cortisol and epinephrine into her large muscle groups, her heart, and her lungs. Legs and arms shaking marks a beginning to return to homeostasis following a fight or flight response.

5.   Hypoaroused. The major flight/flight response is complete but the discrete trauma remains in her body such that she has moved from hyperarousal to hypoarousal with mild dissociation. Effective responses for Lucia after the accident would be to make contact with a supportive person who would tell her she is okay, that she is in good hands, and to let her body do what it needs to, i.e., let the shaking in her arms and legs happen, let any tears come, or let other movement in her body complete.

Chapter 5: Exercise (page 39):

1.   Hypoaroused; 2. Hypoaroused; 3. Hyperaroused; 4. Hyperaroused; 5. Regulated; 6. Hyperaroused; 7. Regulated; 8. Hypoaroused; 9. Hyperaroused; 10. Hypoaroused

Chapter 7: Exercise (page 58):

1.   Psychoanalysts saw attachment as a function of the child's need for food. Bowlby saw the caregiver's attention and emotional approach to the infant/child as key; 2. c and d; 3. babbling, cooing, reaching, following, smiling, crying, sucking, clinging; 4. the imprinting of ducklings; 5. a. secure: relieved to see caregiver, soothed easily, and returns to play soon; b. anxious-ambivalent (preoccupied for adults): shows ambivalence, resists, may hit and pull

away; c. anxious-Avoidant (avoidant/dismissing for adults): may run away, doesn't cling when picked up, may look away; d. disorganized: contradictory behavior; stereotyped behaviors such as rocking, hitting self.

Chapter 8: Chart Exercise (page 70):

1. Dismissing. 2. Dismissing or Disorganized. 3. Disorganized. 4. Disorganized. 5. Secure. 6. Dismissing. 7. Disorganized. 8. Preoccupied. 9. Secure. 10. Dismissing. 11. Preoccupied or Disorganized. 12. Dismissing. 13. Preoccupied .14. Disorganized. 15. Dismissing. 16. Preoccupied. 17. Preoccupied. 18. Dismissing. 19. Dismissing. 20. Secure. 21. Could be any of the insecure attachment strategies. An anxious person might be using/abusing alcohol (a depressant) to regulate a chronically hyperactivating nervous system; a dismissing person might be using/abusing stimulants to enliven a deactivating nervous system.

Chapter 10: Post-Test (page 90):

1. Secure attachment is the primary system as it is the system that is utilized when there is normal growth and development of the self in relationship. Secondary systems are strategies of regulation adopted as needed to cope with attachment insecurity.

2. False.

3. Birth—two years; adolescence

4. Secure attachment protects us as it creates automatic and autonomic responses to threat and danger that will result in the maximum safety possible. Our nervous systems, if we are secure, are primed to accurately appraise and react to real threat/danger, to recover quickly, to seek safety through caregivers, and to return to homeostasis with appropriate relational and other resourcing. Insecure attachment places obstacles in this normal process of

regulation and can therefore leave the person over-responding or under-responding to danger. These responses can create secondary dangers and/or chronic psychological and physical disorders.

5. Brain Structures: a. brainstem, b. neocortex, c. limbic system, d. limbic system e. primarily neocortex combined with integration of all three systems. Integration Processes: a. right-brain vertical integration, b. right-left brain horizontal integration, c. right-brain vertical integration, d. right-brain vertical integration, e. right-left brain horizontal integration, f. right-left brain horizontal integration.

6. The Vagus Nerve.

7. Myelinated = Ventral Vagus; Nonmyelinated = Dorsal Vagus.

8. Internal stress when infant is distressed; mother-eze, looking at the infant; smiling; laughing; repeating what the infant utters; cooing.

9. Stress tolerance; tolerance of a broad range of emotions; ability to take risks; trust that the world is safe; ability to love and connect with relative ease; empathy and compassion for self and others; positive sense of self and others.

10. First two years: implicit memory; procedural learning; unconscious sense of self and others; after first two years: language, thinking, appraising. 1. Right 2. Left.

11. True.

Chapter 13: Exercise (page 102):

Client 1: (not in mindfulness)

a. Voice Quality: speeds up, slows, quiets, loses energy at end of sentence.

b. Energy: mutable; sense of coming forward, moving away.

c. Congruence: smiling and nodding while speaking quickly, voice dissipating, inconsistent eye contact while talking about something difficult.

d. Eye Contact: not maintained after speaking.

e. Movement: nodding head, imperceptible kicking, sitting forward in chair

Continue to track for: safety; responses to your interventions that increase or decrease safety; changes in all of the above as the session continues.

Client 2: (Client not in mindfulness)

f. Physical Reactions to Each other: She looks at him and holds her breath while he is talking, has tight body posture; he does not look at her and is turned away from her, voice gets louder as he speaks.

g. Breathing Patterns: She holds breath while he speaks.

h. Regulation/Dysregulation: His rising voice and flushed face might indicate some hyperarousal. By contrast, her body posture, fixed eye contact, held breath could possibly reflect a dissociative reaction.

i. Voice Quality: His raised and getting louder voice.

j. Eye Contact: His eyes look above her face; her eyes fixed on him.

Continue to track for: Signs of dysregulation in either partner in response to physical reactions and stated content on the part of the other; moments of safe connection; how each responds to you compared to how they respond to the other.

Chapter 13: Exercise (page 103):

Client 1: (Client in mindfulness—1st part)

a. Shifts: changes in breathing, loosening of hand clasp, stated experience of change in lightness in chest.

b. Voice Quality: soft voice when chest feeling lightens.

c. Body States/Movements: breathing into sigh, clasped hands, awareness of chest feeling changed.

Client 1: (Client in mindfulness—2nd part)

    d. Facial expressions/movements: eyes squeezed tight, tears forming, wipes away tears, eyes open.

    e. Congruence: starting to cry, doesn't want to—opens his eyes.

    f. State of Consciousness: somewhat in mindfulness, pops out deliberately.

Client 2: (Client in mindfulness—1st part)

    g. Voice Quality: agitated, possibly trailing off at end.

    h. Quality of Narrative: slightly disjointed, moving back and forth in story, speaking as if in memory.

    i. Quality of Speech: voice agitated, may start loud then get softer as she moves into memory of mother's face close to hers.

    j. Regulation/Dysregulation: possible hypoarousal as she may be more in memory than in dual awareness indicated by moving around in the narrative, then trailing off at end.

Client 2: (Client in mindfulness—2nd part)

    k. Regulation/Dysregulation: becomes quiet, body still, head dropping, tight hands against sides.

    l. Body state/Position: body still, hands tight against her sides.

    m. Energy: seems caught, collapsed, almost frozen.

    n. Shifts: talking to being quiet, head turning and dropping, sense of energy decreasing.

Chapter 14: Exercise (page 108):

Client 1 (1st part): Choices a, b and f are all good choices. Choice c is a little interpretive. Choices d and e both take him away from his current somatic experience into a different realm (emotional or cognitive).

Client 1 (2nd part): Choice a is a directive that might be necessary if the client is dysregulated. Choice b and d are literal contact statements that could be useful depending on level of regulation. Choices c and e are the best as they reflect the overall experience of the client at the moment.

Client 2 (1st part): Choice a is story-based and misses all other fields of experience. Choices c and e are literal contact statements that reflect part of the client's experience. Choice d focuses only on the emotional field and ignores all the energetic and somatic information. Choice b is the best as it expresses the present moment somatic, energetic experience of the client.

Client 2 (2nd part): Choice a is appropriate if you have determined there is dysregulation. Choices b and d are literal contact statements that catch a part of the current experience. Choice c is good although it still misses the intensity and depth of the experience. Choice e is the best choice to reflect what the client is going through at the moment.

Chapter 15: Exercise (page 113):

Possible contact statements: "Things are moving fast, huh?"; "Would it be okay to slow things down a little?"; "How would it be to slow things down?"; "I notice you are talking quickly."

Chapter 16: Exercise (page 120):

1. Choice c and d support the defense; a challenges it; b is an interpretation and misses the importance of the defense in that moment.

2. Choice a is an interpretation; b acknowledges the impact of the therapist response on the client and offers what might be a necessary repair. With c, the therapist backs off out of the client's way without a complete repair; d is wordy but provides psychoeducation about working somatically. Any of these except "a" could be fine depending on the given client and therapist relationship.

3. Both c and d are appropriate responses; a and b do not support the defense or is an interpretation.

Chapter 17: Exercise (page 125):

1. "What happens in the rest of your body when your voice is rushed?"

2. "Is it okay to stay with this and let your hand keep moving in circles?"

3. "Go ahead and just see yourself in the room, exactly where you are, what you are wearing, what else you see."

4. "Let yourself feel the soft friction of your thumb moving across your hand, the warmth…"

5. "Can you describe the tension a little more? Is it painful? Dull? Spreading?

6. "What happens in your body when I acknowledge that?"

Chapter 19: Exercise (page 133):

Client 2: 1. head dropping, 2. agitation of voice as she is talking, 3. voice trails off, 4. rigidity and stillness of body, 5. use of present tense as if she is actually in the memory and not in the present moment.

- Statement to verify: "What age are you now?"
- Statement after confirmation: "Oh, you are five. Can you feel me being here with you?"
- Delivery change: Voice softer, slightly more lilting, sentences short, tenderly solicitous.
- Is client dysregulated? All the possible answers to the first question above would apply here plus client not responding with an observing consciousness. If client is in a child state but can also be aware they are, there is not necessarily dysregulation as they have dual awareness.
- If client is dysregulated: Ask client to open eyes, assess for hyperarousal or hypoarousal, use appropriate resourcing such as looking around the room, naming objects they see, paying attention to body sensation, feeling muscle groups, etc.

Chapter 20: Exercise (page 137):

- New belief: "Just notice what happens in your body when you say that."
- Hand on chest: "Your hand is on your chest. Really let yourself feel into your hand on your chest, that sense of slowing down there and anything else that goes along with it."
- Integrate: "Imagine going back into your life now with this new belief and your hand on your chest. Imagine memorizing all of this and notice how that feels."

Chapter 22: Post-Test (page 153):

1. b. 2. d. 3. "Fright without solution." 4. False, 5. a, d, and g. 6. The "Attachment Bubble" means tracking your own and a client's attachment tendency/system on a moment-to-moment basis so you can understand client responses, intervene appropriately and return yourself to a secure place while working.

CEU Opportunity — Evaluation and Exam

―――――――

CEU EXAMINATION

Six Continuing Education Units are available for completing the workbook for any California LCSW or MFT. You can complete the exam and evaluation online through my website, www. karenrachels.com, and submit payment of $25 through PayPal. Alternatively, you can complete the exam and evaluation below and mail them to me with a $25 check. Contact me at bodybrainlove@gmail.com for mailing information. Depending on the method chosen, I will either email or mail you a certificate of completion.

Please complete the following multiple choice questions. You must pass the exam by 70%. You will have a maximum of three opportunities to pass the exam.

Name: _____ Address: _____
Email: _____ CA License # _____ Phone _____

1. In a somatic attachment approach, therapy aims to:
   a. Increase the client's conscious orientation toward the path to safety.
   b. Increase the amount of time a client spends in the Window of Tolerance.
   c. Decrease defenses.
   d. Both a and b.

2. A young female client you have been seeing for three months reports to you she had a nightmare last night that is still with her. Her hands are fidgety, her face is flushed, and the words appear to come out in torrents. She is:

    a. Hyperaroused

    b. Hypoaroused

    c. Disorganized

    d. Regulated

3. What intervention might you immediately choose for this client?

    a. Focus her attention on her breathing out through exhalation.

    b. Focus her attention on bringing breath in.

    c. Ask her to describe the nightmare more slowly.

    d. Reassure her the nightmare is not actually happening and she is safe.

4. Which brain structure functions as the alarm bell when threat or danger is perceived?

    a. Hippocampus

    b. Thalamus

    c. Middle Prefrontal Cortex

    d. Amygdala

5. What are the two goals of Somatic Attachment Therapy?

    a. Developing a coherent narrative and earning a secure attachment.

    b. Increasing body awareness and decreasing preoccupied thinking.

    c. Improving the client's self-esteem and developing secure interpersonal skills.

    d. Resolving internal conflicts and developing a sense of choice in behavior.

6. What is the essential message of the Polyvagal Theory?

    a. We are most of the time at the mercy of our evolutionary response to danger.

    b. The Vagus Window is a resource for hypoarousal or hyperarousal.

    c. The ventral vagal circuit is responsible for dissociation and freezing.

    d. Humans can manage real and perceived threats or danger through the path to safety.

7. Johnno is talking comfortably with you about his successes at his workplace. He begins to describe a problem he has with a co-worker. You reflect to him, "You felt ashamed." He responds, "So, I'm getting a special award from the company for my work on the new prototype." What attachment system was activated?
   a. Hyperactivating
   b. Deactivating
   c. Hypoaroused
   d. Hyperaroused

8. In the Adult Attachment Interview, a person with this kind of attachment tendency describes their childhood in glowing terms.
   a. Secure
   b. Preoccupied
   c. Avoidant/Dismissing
   d. Disorganized

9. A client is talking about her upcoming wedding. She is smiling, waving her hands and talking quickly. Pick the best contact statement:
   a. You are waving your hands as you talk.
   b. There's a lot of energy here.
   c. You're happy, huh?
   d. How do you feel about getting married?

10. The same client later in the session starts describing her concern about her grandfather. She is worried he will get drunk and be inappropriate. As she is talking, she makes a slight tapping gesture on her chest. You contact the gesture and make which of the following deepening one interventions?
    a. This feels familiar, huh?
    b. Just let yourself feel the rhythm of your fingertips as they touch your chest, notice the energy in your fingers…

    c. The tapping feels good, huh?

    d. Let yourself breathe.

11. What is the most important thing to remember about using touch with a client?

    a. Never use touch if you yourself are not comfortable doing it or you are dysregulated.

    b. Only use touch with a specific purpose in mind, a sense of what is likely to happen and with initial and continual permission of the client.

    c. If the client says yes to a suggestion of touch, be sure to track closely to make sure the yes is accurate and, if so, tell the client exactly what you are doing at any given moment, again tracking closely to make sure the touch is safe.

    d. All of the above.

12. What is the most important thing to remember about making "mistakes" or having empathic breaks with a client?

    a. Secure attachment is built partly on ruptures with clients that are met with ready and sincere repairs.

    b. Anyone can make a mistake.

    c. Empathic breaks are usually a result of a client's attachment tendency.

    d. Self-disclosure can hinder adequate repair.

13. What percentage of people in the United States has a secure attachment?

    a. 20%

    b. 10% – 15%

    c. 5%

    d. 55% - 65%

14. Which of the following is a secondary attachment system?

    a. Secure

    b. Ambivalent

    c. Hyperactivating

    d. Disoriented

15. What is the purpose of mindfulness in Somatic Attachment Therapy?

    a. Progressive relaxation

    b. Observation of internal experience

    c. Establishing emotional security

    d. Reducing suffering

16. What is not a function of the parasympathetic nervous system?

    a. Fight

    b. "Rest and digest"

    c. Social engagement

    d. Physical/emotional homeostasis

17. Which of the following is unique to humans?

    a. Reptilian brain

    b. Limbic system

    c. Neocortex

    d. Brain stem

18. In the Strange Situation, a child who moves back and forth towards and away from mother when mother returns has which attachment style?

    a. Secure

    b. Disorganized

    c. Anxious-Ambivalent

    d. Anxious-Avoidant

19. What information do we gain access to by tracking what is happening in a client's body?

    a. Neocortical insight

    b. Emotional process

    c. Values

    d. Limbic system "hidden layers"

20. When treating a client who has experienced trauma, what is crucial to re-member?

    a. A traumatic event always leads to PTSD.

    b. A client needs to tell the story many times in order to defuse its intensity.

    c. Treating trauma without paying attention to regulation can be re-trau-matizing.

    d. Trauma is a normal part of everyday human experience.

21. When working with a client you think might have an avoidant tendency, what do you need to keep in mind?

    a. The client might spend time storytelling without a lot of connection to feelings.

    b. You might feel bored or disconnected from the client.

    c. The client may readily feel shame.

    d. All of the above.

22. The brain of a 2-year-old is roughly what percentage of a 10-year-old brain?

    a. 75%

    b. 10%

    c. 50%

    d. 25%

23. During a session, in mindfulness, a client states, "A wall just came up." What is the best intervention to use?

    a. "Is it okay to just let the wall be there?"

    b. "What do you think is behind that wall?"

    c. Gently, "Are you afraid of exploring this?"

    d. "Should we stop?"

24. Which of the following represents the use of the "Attachment Bubble"?

    a. You notice yourself tensing when a client gets upset with you and work to ground yourself to stay present and secure.

    b. Despite a client's subtle devaluation of you, you recognize their attachment need to distance you to avoid vulnerability and shame.

    c. You remain empathetic and gentle while setting a frame-related boundary with a client who tends to use preoccupied strategies.

    d. All of the above.

25. Why is it neurobiologically important for an adolescent to have supportive, secure teachers and parents?

    a. Adolescence is a "sensitive" period where the limbic system predominates.

    b. Adolescents tend to abuse drugs.

    c. Adolescents are rebelling.

    d. Adolescents are susceptible to peer pressure.

Course Evaluation

Body, Brain, Love: A Therapist's Workbook for Affect Regulation and Somatic Attachment

Category	Excellent	Very Good	Good	Fair	Poor
Clarity of material					
Usefulness for job skills					
Knowledge of author					
Quality reflects current professional expectations					
Upholds legal/ ethical professional standards					
Adequate graphics/case material					
Satisfaction of goals stated in beginning of book					

Strengths of this workbook: _____

_____

Weaknesses of this workbook: _____

_____

Additional Comments: _____

_____

_____

DVD Ordering Information

A DVD designed to accompany this workbook will be completed by April, 2015. The DVD will include one full Somatic Attachment Therapy session plus demonstrations of the following skills:

- Mindfulness Induction
- Resourcing a Hyperaroused Client
- Resourcing a Hypoaroused Client
- Tracking and Contacting
- Deepening One
- Supporting the Wisdom of Defenses
- Slowing
- Deepening Two
- Use of Touch
- Meaning, Anchoring, and Integration
- Working with a Child State
- Working with a Hyperactivating System
- Working with a Deactivating System

To place an order for a DVD, send an email to Karen Rachels, bodybrainlove@gmail.com, with your name, address, phone number, and email. Or, you can check my website, www.karenrachels.com, to order online.

Credits and Acknowledgments

First and foremost, I'd like to thank Jackie Brookman for her encouragement and persistence in making this workbook happen. As a student in my first class, and as a participant in a practice group, Jackie always had the vision of what this could be and helped me in significant ways along the road.

Brad Reynolds was my graphic designer and formatted the book. In addition to his skills and his artistic eye, Brad had valuable information to offer me about the book writing and publishing process. His advice was always helpful, including suggestions on content at times that enhanced the material.

Claudia Norby, a skillful reader and careful editor, put significant effort into making the workbook more consistent and understandable.

I am grateful to Terry Toth, widow of Ron Kurtz, for granting me permission to utilize some of the foundational Hakomi concepts in the somatic skills section. Donna Martin, Hakomi therapist and trainer, generously gave me her time and thoughts in reviewing the material.

Various people gave me permission to use graphics and information, including Matt McKay of New Harbinger Publications; Mario Mikulincer, attachment researcher and author; Janina Fisher, Sensorimotor Psychotherapy trainer and consultant; Bonnie Badenoch, psychotherapist and neuroscience/attachment author; and Ravi Dykema, online journalist.

Scott Eaton and Julie Murphy, my Hakomi teachers, taught me a great deal about embodying the work I was doing. I am grateful for their patience with my impatience with myself. Michael Quirke and Marty Cooper, colleagues in a short-term neuroscience study group, helped with conceptualizing important material.

A special thanks to Kathy Smith who was a moral and practical support throughout this unfolding process. In addition to helping me teach my classes, she also edited the workbook, gave me content feedback, and wrote a valuable case example for the workbook. Pamarie Pedjoe and Kathy, as assistant teachers, added immeasurably to my understanding of how to teach this material, as did my students and members of my practice group.

I received multiple levels of support from Sandy Vaughn as well as from consultees in my consultation groups. Rebecca Silverstein and Alissa Blackman, two talented therapists, enriched the texture of the workbook by demonstrating clinical applicability through their vignettes.

Like all therapists, I am most indebted to the clients who have engaged with me as my therapeutic style and approach have changed. As a therapist who has also been a client, I am aware of the incredible trust clients put in us to hold them in their vulnerability and in their strength. I have learned and continue to learn from my clients and am grateful they have let me into their lives.

Karen Rachels, MFT
Oakland, CA

Lightning Source UK Ltd.
Milton Keynes UK
UKOW04f1034241016
285994UK00006B/408/P